I0813272

The mantle of leadership can be heavy. Nothing, however, outweighs the cross. Jesus led with such power and clarity that it changed the world. It changed you. Dr. Moore will help you dive deep into Jesus' leadership strategy. This book will empower you to carry your load well and, perhaps, change your own world.

Matt Chandler, elder and lead pastor, The Village Church

As a CEO aiming to integrate my faith into the business world, I can say that *The Master Leader* offers a valuable guide for pursuing excellence and displaying leadership qualities inspired by Jesus. Typically, these qualities are viewed as conflicting, but this book illustrates how together they optimize results. I am convinced that this resource can benefit leaders striving to lead with intention and purpose.

John K. Solheim, president and CEO, Ping Golf

If you're a leader, you're a reader. So many books on leadership may fill your shelf. Why add another? Because this one baptizes leadership wisdom in the life that Jesus lived. It adds the critical lens of Scripture to the common view of leadership principles. It will grow your faith as well as accelerate your leadership.

Kyle Idleman, senior pastor, Southeast Christian Church

If you're like me, your shelves are overflowing with leadership books. But before you decide you don't need another one, I urge you to dig into this tool from two authors who offer tremendous wisdom based on the example of our leader, Jesus. In these pages, you will find both big-picture principles and practical tools that can have a lasting impact on your ministry.

Nancy Beach, leadership coach and author

This book will bolster your commitment to leading with excellence, something that is not easy to accomplish. I love how Mark and Jeff take a serious look at how Jesus led, which is spiritual gold for the leader who bows the knee to Jesus.

Doug Crozier, CEO, The Solomon Foundation

As an executive leader over the past two decades, I've prayed for guidance on how to navigate the many challenges I face daily to ensure I stay true to my faith and don't lose sight of who I am. *The Master Leader* was an answer to my prayers. This book is a great leadership playbook with practical and sound advice that will enable any leader, whether new to leadership or a seasoned veteran, to grow in leadership and lead like Jesus at the same time. I wish I had read this playbook sooner.

Jim Brady, COO of a Fortune 250 company

The Master Leader is a book that truly stands out in the crowded field of leadership resources. This book, focused on the twelve Master Leader values and actions, provides a unique and powerful perspective by juxtaposing these well-worn truths with the life of Jesus. I highly recommend this book to anyone looking to grow as a leader and bring positive change to their organization and community.

Julie Laulis, president, CEO, and chair of the board,
Cable One, Inc.

Having just finished a PhD in Business Administration, I'm wondering, *Why didn't they just make me read this book?* It would have been so much more helpful. *The Master Leader* will help you figure out how to think, be, and lead like Jesus. Isn't that what life is all about anyway? Loved all the practical tools and action steps.

Doug Lucas, president, TeamExpansion.org

To be influential leaders of faith who aspire to make a meaningful impact, we must first decide how we want to influence others and the way we want to go about it. *The Master Leader* is the "how-to" book for leading like Jesus. This book provides both foundational and practical direction for embodying effective Christian leadership.

Pastor John K. Jenkins Sr., senior pastor,
First Baptist Church of Glenarden

Mark and Jeff provide sage advice in their book, *The Master Leader*, which applies to all leaders, whether people of deep faith or leaders in the secular world. Jeff's extensive resume as a Fortune Global 500 company leader, a CEO, and now a pastor, gives him the experience to understand the role that leadership values and culture play in the success of any organization. This book is a must read for those seeking to become trusted leaders of highly successful organizations.

Alan Yordy, past president, CEO, and
Chief Mission Officer, PeaceHealth

As Christian leaders, we are often tempted to separate our faith from our leadership practices in fear that one weakens the other. *The Master Leader* is a roadmap to embracing a faith that enhances our leadership effectiveness when we cast a vision and build a culture based on integrity and consistency. Thanks to Mark and Jeff for the real-world examples that encourage us to do so.

Milton Boyer, pharmaceutical executive

The challenge of being a CEO and a Christian is not only lonely but also a constant struggle under the world's view of both. *The Master Leader* helps me know I am not alone in this journey, giving practical, Christian-focused leadership and guidance in a much-needed book. I've known Jeff Osborne for many years, and his ability to put Christ first and apply caring decisions to his organizations is admirable.

Jeff Ellington, president and CEO, Runbeck Election Services

This book is what business leaders and church leaders need! Jeff provides helpful tools to get you started—*the how*—and Mark provides biblical truths from the Holy Scripture—*the why*. These two thought leaders have prepared your agenda to become the Master Leader you were made to be!

Ken Bohlen, former pastor (Scottsdale, Arizona);
retired Chief Innovation Officer, Textron, Inc.

Being a business owner and Christian leader can be a lonely place. Finding true mentorship that understands the challenges that come with both can be very difficult. Mark and Jeff not only talk the talk, but they also walk the walk. These two men have not only challenged me to be a better leader, but they have also challenged me to be a better Christian leader. *The Master Leader* will help you know you are not alone in this journey and provide practical principles and actions that can be applied in any leadership role.

Richard Dickens, founder and former CEO,
Dickens Quality Demolition

So many times we struggle as Christian leaders with how to live out our faith in the marketplace, and *The Master Leader* gives us practical and sound advice on how to do just that. Mark and Jeff have given us practical leadership examples and biblical principles to help us put our faith into action as leaders. You will love this read!

Steve Lanter, CEO, Lanter Delivery Systems

With the heavy call of leadership, we all need a clear playbook on how to lead well and how to lead like Jesus. *The Master Leader provides* a road map for achieving both objectives. This book is a game-changer for leaders.

Dr. Lori Maldonado, CEO, Teach One to Lead One

This book is a must read for any Christian leader. I appreciated the practical principles focused on building culture, which is critical for any organization looking to pass the test of time and make a transformational kingdom and community impact. This book can serve as a great guide for any level of leader, and I can't wait for my entire leadership team to go through it!

Dr. Ryan Senters, CEO, Ohana;
host of the *Unleash Your Purpose* podcast

THE MASTER LEADER

12 WAYS TO LEAD LIKE JESUS

MARK E. MOORE

WITH JEFF OSBORNE

Nashville, Tennessee

HIM Publications

The Master Leader

Requests for information should be sent via email to HIM Publications. Visit himpublications.com for contact information.

A previous version of this book was published as *Master Leader* by College Press (2018).

All emphases in Scripture quotations and other quotations are the authors'.

Library of Congress Control Number: 2024937048

ISBN: 978-1-970102-75-8 (Paperback)
ISBN: 978-1-970102-76-5 (Hardback)
ISBN: 978-1-970102-77-2 (ePub)

Editorial and art direction: Chad Harrington (YouPublish.com)
Cover and interior design: Bryana Anderle (YouPublish.com)

To the two leaders who impacted my leadership journey more than any others: Ken Idleman, former president of Ozark Christian College in Joplin, Missouri; and Don Wilson, founding pastor of Christ's Church of the Valley in Phoenix, Arizona.

— *Mark E. Moore*

Leadership is all about influence. No one influenced me more than my father, Duane Osborne. Thanks for being the most significant influence in my life. To my wife, Pam, who lives out leadership better than anyone I know. Thanks for always being the wind beneath my wings—without you, my leadership journey simply wouldn't have happened.

— *Jeff Osborne*

CONTENTS

THE MAKING OF A MASTER LEADER

John Maxwell says, "Everything rises and falls on leadership."[1] I've tried to argue with that, since it is an absolute statement and absolute statements are seldom true. I've tried. But I can't think of an exception to that rule in any organization, whether civic, religious, or business. Leadership is the fuel of human flourishing in families, churches, tribes, and nations. It appears that this is by God's design. It was a king who wrote, "The LORD is my shepherd" (Ps. 23:1). He led the nation; God led the king. In Romans 13:1, the great theologian Paul wrote, "Let every person be subject to the governing authorities. For there is no authority except from God, and those that exist have been instituted by God." God designed and designated leaders to care for the world he created.

When leaders carry out God's will and shepherd his people, the flock flourishes. Not only does everything rise and fall on leadership, but all leaders are God's leaders, even those who are not godly. Some attain power to guide and guard God's people, such as David and Moses. Some are raised up by God for discipline or retribution, such as Nebuchadnezzar or Caesar. If you are in leadership, whether in a church, business, or government, it is because God put his hand on you and expects (even demands) you to carry out his will.

If it is your desire to lead on behalf of the Good Shepherd, then this book is for you. I have spent my professional career chasing hard after Jesus. For more than two decades, I taught a course called "The Life of Christ" at Ozark Christian College. Since 2012, I have been a teaching pastor for Christ's Church of the Valley in Phoenix, Arizona, working with leaders in churches, businesses, and nonprofits. My purpose in writing this book is to introduce you to the leadership principles of Jesus and how they apply to your own leadership context. However, I have never been the point leader of an organization. So to authentically apply these biblical principles, I have asked a colleague of mine to join this project.

Allow me to introduce Jeff Osborne. He has worked as a C-level leader in multiple organizations and has coached hundreds of leaders in the business world. He came on staff with Christ's Church of the Valley in 2020 as one of our executive pastors. Jeff's career "crossover" makes him the ideal collaborator. In each chapter, I've asked him to address a key question from a C-level leader's seat. His perspective will be invaluable as you apply the principles of Jesus. I invite you to hear part of Jeff's story.

As Mark mentioned, my journey of leadership has been filled with successes, failures, and—most of all—lessons. As I share some of these lessons with you in this book, let me start by sharing one of the most important lessons, which is to have the proper leadership mindset.

It was an excellent operational model. I presented it with such conviction. As I sat back down at the intimidating, oversized table in our executive boardroom, the heads of our business division politely nodded and thanked me. Following my presentation, a colleague offered an alternative plan. He received a rousing round of applause.

I had a pit in my stomach. *He won. I lost.*

You can see the problem. We were on the same team. I chose a scarcity mindset over an abundance mindset. For years, that soundtrack ran on repeat in my head. I'm embarrassed to admit that more than a few times after that meeting, I wished ill on my colleague—that he would fail.

This scarcity mindset robbed me of collaborating with this leader and sharing ideas that would make both our divisions great. I could have celebrated his success and worked to raise my game. We probably could have done some great things together.

Since those days, I've worked hard to lead with an abundance mindset, to be a more mature and confident leader who believes there is room for all of us to be successful. Our mindset matters. That's what this book is all about.

Before we manage others, we must first master the management of ourselves. And that requires a strong and healthy leadership mindset. We must determine the type of leader we want to be—a critical step in leading like the Master. Settle it now: *What kind of leader do I want to become?* One of the best ways to think about this might be to ask yourself: *What do I want my leadership brand to say about me and how I lead others? What do I want to be known for as a leader?*

Often, the problem with leadership isn't that we don't know how to lead, but rather, that we haven't clarified the leadership brand for which we want to be known. We simply wing it. I think you'll agree that when it comes to leadership, "winging it" isn't a great strategy. Effective and influential leadership demands that we consider deeply the desired impact of our leadership.

We all know leaders whom we deem to be great or who have had significant impact on our lives. We just don't often think about *why* they were able to make that level of impact and how we might be able to have a similar effect. Often, we are too busy focusing on the "doing" aspect of leadership and fulfilling our responsibilities to worry about who we are as a leader.

We need Jesus' model of leadership. Leading like Jesus is not as difficult as it may seem! We have so many examples of both good and bad leaders from a myriad of sources—Scripture, the marketplace, history, and personal experience. Once we develop the values of a Master Leader and begin to act on the values and actions Jesus taught and showed us, we'll be well on our way to becoming Master Leaders.

To adopt the right leadership mindset—the mindset of Jesus—we must think strategically about the attributes, styles, characteristics, and values we want to exercise in our own personal leadership. This all takes time, focus, and energy—valuable resources few of us have in abundance. What can we do? The first half of the battle of leadership is fought between our ears.

When I was a young, inexperienced leader and wanted to grow in my leadership, I would sit in meetings with high-level leaders and think about how they would respond to a question or a situation. At first, I would get about half the answers right. Over time, it was closer to 75 percent. Eventually, I was able to think like the leaders above me. This mindset training required me to be present in the moment and not merely half-listening to the leadership exchange taking place around me.

Being intentional about the mindset we want to possess as leaders is a helpful exercise for our "leadership muscles." Our mindset ensures we have spent time thinking through how we want to lead before we find ourselves in the middle of a situation where we can easily be caught off guard. Ask yourself: *Do I want to be a leader who's known for getting things done, or do I want to be a leader who's known for equipping and empowering others to do great things? Do I want to be a leader others fear or follow? Do I want to be a leader who always has the right answer, or a leader who listens generously to feedback?* When you choose the type of leader you want to be, you create a mindset and a mental map to set the course you'll follow as you lead others. As Christians, Jesus is our model for becoming a Master Leader.

Determining our leadership mindset requires us to be mindful of each situation, which simply means that our leadership style and approach will need to ebb and flow depending on the situation and the people we lead. Most church leaders strive to be servant leaders—providing encouragement, delegating well, or empowering their team. Though we all aspire to be this type of leader, many situations require us to direct, tell, and guide our team, spending less time on collaborating and coaching. Great leaders master servanthood, flexibility, and nimbleness. The best leaders know how to fly at different altitudes depending on the situations or challenges they are required to manage. Determine the kind of leader you desire to be, but remember that leadership is a journey—a muscle group, if you will—and that it will require constant attention, training, and investment to achieve excellence.

How to Use This Book

Jeff and I sincerely desire that the twelve Master Leader values and actions in this book empower you to be the kind of leader you are called to be as a disciple of Jesus. If you are leading people in any capacity, you likely have a voracious appetite for leadership resources: books, conferences, websites, and podcasts. Perhaps that's why you picked up this book; you want to grow as a leader. But if you have a line of other leadership books on your shelf, you may be asking, "How is this book any different than the plethora of other offerings?" After all, a wise man once said, "There is nothing new under the sun" (Eccl. 1:9). Sure enough, the values and actions in these pages are well-worn truths. What makes them unique in this context is their juxtaposition to the life of Jesus.

Our goal is to tie leadership principles to the model of Jesus. After all, he is literally the founding father of servant leadership. Prior to him, there were no leaders who practiced servant leadership or philosophers who advocated for it. By tracing the teachings of Jesus, as well as his actions, we can sleuth the origin of the heart and habits of the Master Leader.

The title of this book, *The Master Leader*, goes back to the fact that Jesus was the greatest leader of all time. Starting with just a small number of disciples, Jesus made more of an impact on humanity than anyone else in history. He embodied the twelve leadership values and actions of this book better than anyone. Our prayer for this book is that these twelve leadership principles will empower you to have a greater impact than you ever imagined.

Your impact will be in direct proportion to your allegiance to the Master and alignment with him. He's not merely our personal Master. He is *the* Master Leader, unmatched in history. Whereas one of my previous books, *Core 52*, focused on fifty-two Bible passages, this book focuses on twelve leadership principles. Both books, in different ways, point squarely to Jesus, the author and perfecter of our faith.

Standard leadership books focus on core pillars such as identity, vision, mission, values, strategies, and stewardship. This book will filter these through the model of Jesus. Whether you lead a church, a ministry, a nonprofit organization, or a marketplace venture, if you want to lead like Jesus, this book will help you identify the original values and actions of the Master and apply them in a contemporary context.

I've broken the book into two main parts. Part 1, "The Values of a Master Leader" (chapters 1 through 6), looks at six characteristics of a Christian leader, and Part 2 looks at the actions of a Master Leader—how those values can be practiced in the rough and tumble of our leadership roles.

Leadership begins with *integrity* (chapter 1), not merely doing the right thing, but being the right person. Who we are comes from what we believe about ourselves. When we look at the life of Jesus, we discover that his integrity came from his revolutionary idea that God was his Father. His Father's love, approval, and calling gave him the courage to live consistently according to God's agenda. This can be you too. The second characteristic is *servanthood* (chapter 2). Jesus expressed this in his relentless and unique self-designation: "Son of Man." His ability to serve and suffer as the Son of Man came from his confidence in his Father. Chapters 1 and 2 explore our identity as leaders, providing both confidence and humility.

Because Master Leaders are under God's authority, they aren't really *masters*, but servants. They are not rulers who wield power, but *stewards* (chapter 3) of what God has entrusted to them. Jesus demonstrated how to steward all the resources God entrusted to him. It went well beyond material resources to include people, time, and communication. But no one can steward God's resources well without being *consistent* (chapter 4). That comes through habits, what the church fathers called "disciplines." Though we have nothing like a comprehensive list of Jesus' disciplines in the Gospels, what we do have is telling. He addressed two priority habits: prayer and Sabbath. While there are plenty of other habits leaders should master, these two are particularly important to Jesus for leading a life of balance.

In chapter 5 we'll focus on Jesus' primary value of love, which I am calling "*caring*." It drove all his actions, up to the cross. It was the primary command that summarized all the Mosaic law. But values without behaviors are just plaques on a wall. The final character value of a Master Leader is *nimbleness* (chapter 6). By tapping into the shepherding practices of leaders in the Bible, particularly the ones we see through Jesus' ministry, we can see how to move adroitly and adjust with agility to confront the challenges that face the flock.

In Part 2, "The Actions of a Master Leader" (chapters 7 through 12), we examine some tactical behaviors that will grow both the depth and breadth of your church or organization. After all, the health of the group always starts with its leader. We begin in chapter 7 with the specific actions that embedded Jesus' primary value of love into real-world situations through practicing mercy and inclusion. This is precisely how organizations *build culture.*

Chapter 8 addresses *casting vision.* That is your main role as a leader—to cast a compelling vision of a preferred future. Jesus' vision, in a nutshell, was to restore Eden. That is precisely what will happen someday in the new heaven and the new earth. But in the meantime, Jesus set out to bring a bit of heaven to earth as a precursor of things to come. In chapter 9 we look at how we *develop strategy* and how Jesus adopted the shepherding metaphor for his own role. The shepherd's duties are still a good template of what we could (read "must") do in our organizations. Leaders lead, feed, heal, and protect the flock. Developing strategies around those priorities keeps us focused.

In chapter 10 we examine what it looks like to *focus priorities* with Jesus' vision of God's kingdom. His focus models for us the importance of keeping our "main thing" the main thing. His effectiveness shows us the importance of doing less to get more done. In chapter 11 we observe that leaders prefer *taking action* over discussion. So did Jesus. In fact, his final words on earth were a proactive commission, sending his followers to establish his kingdom globally. That's a task larger than any of us, which leads us to our final chapter.

We need to *mentor leaders* (chapter 12). This ultimately means we make our own disciples in order to carry on the mission. Jesus had his Twelve, and they passed the torch to those who traveled with them. Down the line it went, until here we are today.

You are a leader following in the steps of the Master. My goal in writing this book is not simply that you would become a great leader, but that you would be a Master Leader—leading like and leading *for* the one who initiated this whole thing we call servant leadership.

In each chapter, I offer three consistent building blocks, opening each with a tangible example of the principle we are addressing. This will pull the principle from the philosophical ether and ground it in our present reality. My hope is that you can use these stories or ones like them to help your team see the relevance of your training on these topics.

Also, each chapter answers a specific question that leaders face. I invited Jeff, whom I introduced above, to write these sections so you can hear from an experienced leader who has spent significant time leading in the marketplace. You will feel the significance of his contributions in these practical sections of each chapter. He speaks authentically and experientially to the issues you face at the top of your team.

Following Jeff's contribution, I tap into my twenty-two years of Bible college teaching on the life of Jesus, mining for leadership principles. My goal is to summarize and synthesize the jewels of the Master's leadership and present them to you, polished and ready to set in the gold studs of your own leadership setting. We're not just looking for quotes and quips. We are finding patterns in Jesus' leadership that are both repeatable and transferable. This is what sets *The Master Leader* apart from other excellent leadership books. I filter legitimate biblical scholarship through a leadership lens to give you an executive summary of the historical Jesus. Our hope is this approach will help inform and ground you in the values and practices of Jesus that most impact your leadership decisions and leadership style.

As you read, make sure to use the "Take Action" sections at the end of each chapter. You will also find bonus material on some of those exercises, which are available at TheMasterLeader.com/tools. Each of these exercises was carefully culled and analyzed for practical leadership development. We urge you to do more than just read this book and shelve it with the others. These action steps can turn this book into a training manual for leadership development. Consider reading this with your team, a mentoring group, or other leaders with whom you consult, and work through the exercises together. Also, make sure to access the video course and group discussion questions we created to go with this book. Visit TheMasterLeader.com/tools for access. These will help you process the content of this book as a team through supplemental material and dialogue.

Your leadership is a gift from God and a responsibility to him. The marketplace is full of great resources and good advice. Like you, Jeff and I have used and benefited from them. As Christians, however, we have a Master who stands above all kings and CEOs. His path to achievement and success is different, sometimes counterintuitive. To lead like him—to become a Master Leader—doesn't just encompass the highest stakes. It includes the highest privileges.

PART 1

THE VALUES OF A MASTER LEADER

Leadership is more about *who* we are than what we *do*. That's why this book begins with six character values of Jesus, the Master Leader, that we must embrace and imitate to lead like him.

We begin with *integrity* birthed out of an identity found in our heavenly Father. This identity frees us for *servanthood*. This leads to *stewardship*, recognizing we are merely managers for the Father, not owners. Good stewardship requires the discipline of *consistency* in our own habits, *caring* for the children of God, and *nimbleness* for the ever-changing needs and challenges of the flock. These leadership values are the prerequisites to living out the actions of the Master Leader (Part 2). When we get the *who* right, the *how* will more easily follow.

1

INTEGRITY

The thirty-seventh president of the United States was massively successful. He ended a very unpopular war and normalized relations with China. Domestically, he was equally impactful—so powerful that he was reelected by a landslide in 1972. Undoubtedly, he would have gone down in history as one of America's greatest presidents had it not been for a tiny glitch called Watergate.

After Richard Nixon's reelection, the country learned that members of his party had broken into the Democratic National Headquarters to steal information that would help secure his reelection. Though Nixon didn't order the break-in, subsequent audiotapes revealed he was complicit in covering it up. Rather than facing impeachment, Nixon became the first president in U.S. history to resign his office. His name is now synonymous with duplicity and ignominy. Leadership is more than what you do on the public stage. It begins behind the scenes with *who you are when no one is watching.* Integrity is the foundation of trust and is essential to a legacy that lasts.

Richard Nixon's resignation is etched in my memory. I recall watching from a black-and-white TV at a public swimming pool in the summer of 1974. I was eleven years old and as imperceptive as one would expect a tween to be. Even so, I remember thinking, *Oh no! If we can't trust the president, who can we trust?* Nixon didn't merely destroy his own presidency; he irreparably damaged Americans' respect for the office. From that day to this, the esteem of the highest office in the country has diminished precipitously. It would be difficult to overestimate the importance of integrity in leadership. As James Kouzes and Barry Posner say, "If you don't believe in the messenger, you won't believe in the message."[2] So before I answer the question "Where did Jesus' integrity come from?" I want you to hear from Jeff as he speaks to what it means for a leader to have integrity.

What Does It Mean for a Leader to Have Integrity?

Sometimes we think of integrity as synonymous with morality. But it's more than that. Integrity is not just doing the right things; it's being the right person. Simply said, integrity is when the inside aligns with the outside. Ergo, as leaders, we must know what's inside ourselves to have integrity. What are we trying to model in and through our leadership? Leading with integrity requires us to be crystal clear on the standards we want to uphold. And just as important, we must be aware of how our thoughts and actions are aligning to those standards.

As Christian leaders, we know to look to the Bible for the standards we should uphold. Though each of our leadership situations are nuanced and the Bible doesn't always directly address our specific challenges, overarching principles of Scripture are relevant to any situation we find ourselves in. We must identify the standards of integrity we want to live out. These standards will be a combination of attributes we know to be true from Scripture and the examples of what we've seen demonstrated through godly leaders—parents, teachers, coaches, etcetera. Let's be honest: there are very few situations where it's unclear if a leader is acting in ways that align with God's standards.

Are we living out these standards? To be certain, we must develop the muscle group of self-awareness. To do the right thing when no one is looking requires that we look honestly at ourselves first and be honest about what we see.

Over the decades of leading both individuals and organizations, I have realized that self-awareness is one of the most important skills to master. It's also one of the greatest deficiencies in leaders today. Without strong self-awareness, we as leaders often find ourselves in a place of self-deception. We want to do the right thing and truly believe we are doing the right thing, but due to our lack of self-awareness, we can easily fall into feeling like an imposter or poseur, that we are not being genuine to the values we believe to be true. An example of this is when we act like a hard-nosed "tough guy" about a situation in a way we think will impress the leaders around us, but deep inside there is a caring person who wants to show compassion and empathy.

Self-awareness, though simple, is not always easy. It requires us to ask for input, listen generously, and then have the humility to act on the input. In most leadership roles these days, getting feedback is not optional. It comes through performance reviews, one-on-one meetings, engagement surveys, and frank conversations with our leaders, peers, direct reports, family, and friends. The challenge is not just asking for and receiving feedback but also leveraging that feedback into specific meaningful changes in our behaviors. These behaviors become the foundation of being a leader of integrity.

One of the most helpful tools for turning feedback into actionable change is a "blind-spot board." This is nothing more than a list of our top five blind spots that can become liabilities if we don't remain aware of them and counteract them wherever possible. I created a blind-spot board for myself years ago. It is still displayed in my office for two main purposes: 1) to be a keen reminder for me of my blind spots, and 2) to allow my team to see them so they can hold me accountable. Blind spots can cause significant damage if we, as leaders, are unaware of them and do not find ways to mitigate them.

Here are a few examples of blind spots from my board: don't get ahead of the team; listen, pause, respond—don't react; don't let perfection get in the way of progress (GETMO: Good Enough to Move On); spiking the ball on the five-yard line is a fumble, not a touchdown; and always finish.

Our leadership blind spots are not much different than the blind spots we encounter when driving a car. They keep us from seeing potential danger in our periphery. Blind spots cause collisions. The issue is not that we have blind spots (we all do); it's that we don't take time to check our blind spots. As leaders, we tend to focus on our many strengths and not worry about our blind spots. Although we all should lean toward leveraging our strengths first, if we're unaware of our blind spots, we can significantly diminish the effectiveness of our leadership to those we serve. It's just too big a risk to ignore our blind spots.

Now that we are aware of how we are seen by others and of our blind spots, the key to maintaining integrity is to make sure we make the right next choice. Integrity involves knowing the right thing to do and then doing it. When we lead, many of our daily decisions and actions feel isolated or separate from who we are as a leader, but they have a tremendous compounding effect when it comes to integrity. As Christian leaders, there are no small things, no insignificant decisions; there are all big decisions wrapped in small packages.

Jesus often focused on small and seemingly insignificant illustrations to help us understand that there are few decisions or behaviors that don't matter. He reminds us of the significance of a small splinter in our own eye. If we have faith as small as a mustard seed, we can move mountains. A couple of fish and a few loaves can feed thousands. A simple deceit from Ananias about holding back money caused him and his wife to literally drop dead. Because each decision we make creates a ripple effect on those we lead, there are no unimportant or insignificant decisions as a Christian leader. We first must take care to ensure we know how we are behaving with heightened self-awareness and then be diligent to make sure we pay attention to make the right next choice, even in the small things.

Where Did Jesus' Integrity Come From?

Jeff's perspective is invaluable as we turn now to the Gospels. No one questions that Jesus was a man of integrity. He lived his values. He was the same person in private as in public, with the wealthy as with the poor, with morally impeccable religious leaders as with cunning tax collectors. How was it that Jesus managed to have such integrity—to be so integrated in his values? It's no secret. He talked about it frequently. His values, and his value, came from his Father in heaven.

Jesus was the same person in private as in public.

Because Jesus talked so frequently about the Father, speaking about God as our Father feels normal, at least for Christians. In Jesus' age, however, that was a radically revolutionary idea. It changed the landscape of religion. Until Jesus, no one imagined having a personal relationship with God. I would suggest that it is equally revolutionary today and never more needed. Why? Because the greatest barrier to integrity is our fractured identity. Our brokenness creates spiritual confusion when we try to meet competing and inappropriate expectations.

The good news is that Jesus provided a way for us to connect with our heavenly Father. We can find our identity in him as an antidote to the competing voices in the world around us attempting to impose a different identity on us. Therefore, as a starting point for integrity, leaders must find their identity and value in a Father who has already called, equipped, and approved them. That's why we begin our investigation into Jesus' leadership with his own identity.

Jesus' Identity in the Gospels

Throughout the Gospels we see Jesus' sense of intimate and personal connection with the Father. Look at the number of times he references his relationship.

The following chart is a summary of the data:

Jesus Identified God As	Matthew	Mark	Luke	John	Total
"Father"	39	4	22	103	168
"My Father"	18	1	8	44	71

Why does it matter that Jesus perceived himself as God's Son? Because that's where his identity came from. He didn't need the approval of religious leaders. He didn't fear the contagion of sinners. He didn't have to self-promote or fight to protect himself. He was secure in his Father's approval, fully free to live his life and carry out his calling with perfect integration and integrity—personally, professionally, and spiritually. The same can be true of you. By imitating Jesus, your leadership can be freed from inappropriate expectations and demands from others and from yourself.

Jesus' identity as the "Son of God" allowed him to claim his rightful and exalted role without an ounce of arrogance or pride. It allowed him to be in full submission to the Father's authority without fear of losing his own independence. He had both bold confidence and radical humility because of his connection with his Father.

Jesus had confidence and humility because of his connection with his Father.

For years I struggled with my identity and felt the impact it had on my integrity. My father is a good and godly man, but due to his own upbringing and a painful divorce, he struggled with expressing his emotions. I carried that wound for decades. In my college years, I excelled academically, partially out of a desperate need for approval from father figures. In my thirties, I found my professional achievements filling an emotional need that should have come more naturally from my marriage and children. It wasn't until my forties that I began to accept the approval of my heavenly Father. This began to free me from the need for approval, which liberated me for more humble service, transparent vulnerability, and intimate friendships.

This is but a brief glimpse through the window of my own soul that may serve as a mirror to your own. Hopefully, it's a reminder of the impact your identity can have on your integrity. Powerful leaders can be driven by insecurity rather than divine responsibility. Many times I have witnessed how insecurity can jeopardize a leader's integrity, putting their legacy at risk.

To lead with maximized integrity, we must follow Jesus' example and find our identity in being a child of our heavenly Father. As we do this, we can live under the Father's authority, building both confidence and humility, which in turn, empower our integrity.

Below is a sampling of what being under the Father's authority meant for Jesus' ministry. Take a moment to circle or highlight two or three principles that you could implement immediately into your leadership practices to make the most impact most quickly.

1. *Jesus delegated authority based on his Father's revelation:* "I assign to you, as my Father assigned to me, a kingdom, that you may eat and drink at my table in my kingdom and sit on thrones judging the twelve tribes of Israel" (Luke 22:29–30; see also Matt. 16:17–18; 18:19; 20:23).
2. *Jesus prioritized people based on God's priorities:* "See that you do not despise one of these little ones. For I tell you that in heaven their angels always see the face of my Father who is in heaven" (Matt. 18:10; see also Matt. 18:14; John 10:29).
3. *Jesus submitted to suffering because of his Father's will:* "And going a little farther he fell on his face and prayed, saying, 'My Father, if it be possible, let this cup pass from me; nevertheless, not as I will, but as you will'" (Matt. 26:39; see also John 10:18).
4. *Jesus was secure enough in his identity to submit to his Father's will:* "All things have been handed over to me by my Father, and no one knows who the Son is except the Father, or who the Father is except the Son and anyone to whom the Son chooses to reveal him" (Luke 10:22).

5. *Jesus' self-confidence empowered his endurance as he imitated his Father:* "My Father is working until now, and I am working" (John 5:17; see also John 10:37).
6. *Jesus was glorified only by his Father:* "If I glorify myself, my glory is nothing. It is my Father who glorifies me, of whom you say, 'He is our God'" (John 8:54).
7. *Jesus freely communicated what his Father shared with him:* "No longer do I call you servants, for the servant does not know what his master is doing; but I have called you friends, for all that I have heard from my Father I have made known to you" (John 15:15).

Each of these connections with the Father reveals Jesus' integrity as a leader that flowed from his confident identity. Knowing who you are as a leader is of paramount importance. Warren Bennis and Robert Thomas make this observation: "When the 75 members of the Stanford graduate school of businesses advisory council were asked to recommend the most important capability for leaders to develop, their answer was nearly unanimous: self-awareness."[3]

Our Integrity as Leaders

How does all this relate to our integrity as leaders? A common misconception of leadership is that leadership leads to freedom. As you probably know, it does not. Leadership is not "freedom from" but "freedom to." We have the freedom to carry out obligations. It's the people you feel obligated to who will determine your level of integrity. If you feel obligated to an unethical boss, you'll lose integrity. If you feel obligated to your own pride, it will lead to catastrophic mismanagement. If you feel you have multiple competing obligations—family, lust, greed, reputation—you will lose integrity to multiple masters.

For example, leaders are often blinded by the sycophantic praise of their followers who hope to cling to their coattails for success and significance. Church leaders are certainly not immune to this. We are often *more* vulnerable because the praise of men is in the shadow of the Almighty who has ordained us to lead—or so we believe. It's easy to lose ourselves if we're not connected to the Father and obligated first and foremost to him.

If your exclusive obligation is to your heavenly Father, he will not only endow you with his authority; he will also grant you his unmitigated approval. You can, therefore, be free to serve, free to obey, free to give, free to speak hard truths, and free to delegate. It's this "freedom to" that comes from God the Father and brings uncompromised integrity in our leadership.

Chapter Summary

Integrity is the foundation of leadership. It is not just doing the right things; it's being the right person—aligning our actions with God's values. This seems simple enough. However, without a clear view of the Father and close connection to him, the values we want to embody can become mere rules; and rules without relationship typically lead to rebellion. As we come to know the Father, we sense his approval and love. His value of us allows his values to live in us, resulting in a life of integrity. It also develops a deep humility—a humility that enables us to serve others sacrificially. We'll talk about this servanthood in the next chapter.

TAKE ACTION ON INTEGRITY

Jesus' identity was the foundation for his leadership integrity. He had clarity on his relationship with his Father, and that clarity empowered his integrity. It is the same for all Master Leaders following in the Master's footsteps. When we are clear about who we are and our foundation, our integrity can be unfettered from the pressures of our personal or professional stakeholders. With the Father's authority and approval, we can lead with humility and serve with integrity the people God has called us to lead. Here are two actions you can take toward this end.

The Father Index

Uncover the Influence of Your Earthly and Heavenly Fathers

Carve out an hour free from interruptions. Turn off your phone. Open your journal to two blank pages. On the left page, write "Earthly Father" and make three columns: *Descriptors*, *Memories*, and *Gratitude*. Do the same on the right page under the title "Heavenly Father." The columns will look like this:

Descriptors	Memories	Gratitude

For the first twenty-five minutes, write single-word descriptors in the first column that aptly describe your earthly father. These might include words like *caring, distant, sullen, angry, fun, responsible,* or even *absent*. If you did not grow up with an earthly father (or if you had an abusive father), this will be a difficult exercise, and I am sorry if this triggers pain. Be encouraged, however, that this exercise can still drive you to your heavenly Father. You may choose to either leave the first column blank or substitute a father figure from your life who helped shape your identity.

In the middle column under "Memories," briefly summarize important events in your life that you experienced with your earthly father (or didn't have if he was absent or abusive). This could be a camping trip, words of wisdom, habits he had, a moment of discipline, a gift he gave you, or something he taught you. It might help to break up your life into stages: ages one to ten, eleven to eighteen, nineteen to twenty-five, twenty-six to thirty-nine, etcetera. Finally, make a list of things you appreciate about your father under "Gratitude." For example, these could be lessons learned, habits formed, gifts given, or words spoken. You don't have to complete one column before moving to the next. Often, all three columns will explode at once with a memory.

After twenty-five minutes, move to the next page. Do the same as above while thinking of your heavenly Father. Do *not* write what the Bible says about God in the first column. Write only what you have experienced with him. In the middle column, your memories might be (and often will be) arbitrated through a human or group experience. You might have experienced God's provision through a neighbor, his beauty through an artist, or his power in creation, the birth of a child, or corporate worship at church.

For the final ten minutes, compare the lists. Write two summary conclusions: first write one titled "The Way I See God Through the Lens of My Earthly Father," and then write one called "The Way I See God as Different from My Earthly Father." The purpose of this exercise is to clarify and magnify your heavenly Father in your life so that his approval and agenda can drive your identity, because it is your identity that empowers your integrity.

Personal Declaration

Create a Blueprint for Your Identity

Please do not procrastinate on this exercise. Several years ago, I went through a difficult season (partially of my own making). I was considering leaving my ministry. This exercise sustained my ministry through the dark night of the soul. I pray it does the same for you, today or someday—a crisis is always looming for leaders. A personal declaration is a statement about what you believe could and should be true about you. This is both a description of who you are and a promise to yourself of who you will become.

Here are some steps to pull it off:

1. Find a solitary place to think and write without interruption for at least thirty minutes.
2. Imagine yourself at your own funeral. In your mind, watch specific people come up to the front. Listen as they describe what they appreciated about you. Feverishly write down everything you want these important people to say about you at the end of your life.
3. Now organize those thoughts into five to ten deliberate statements (not more than two paragraphs). See my example below.
4. Let that sit overnight. The next day, read what you wrote out loud three or four times and then edit it for clarity.
5. Let it sit overnight again. Repeat the editing process, adding anything important to you and deleting anything unnecessary.
6. Repeat your personal declaration out loud until you have it memorized. Feel free to continue editing it as you say it dozens of times.
7. Recite it out loud every day for a month. Then repeat it at least once a week until your actions align with your intentions.

Here is my personal declaration (in case you would like to get a feel for what might be helpful): "I am spiritually sound, physically fit, mentally sharp, emotionally resilient, and relationally wise. I am inspired by Jesus Christ, empowered by the Holy Spirit, and loved by the Father. Therefore, I can work relentlessly, fight fearlessly, love radically, and serve selflessly. I am a Christian."

This is who I am, partially. It is also the trajectory I am on. By repeating this statement frequently, I keep these priorities in view during my daily activities to create habits that result in the character I want to embody and display. Once again, the purpose of this exercise is to clarify your identity, because it is your identity, more than any other factor, that empowers your integrity.

2

SERVANTHOOD

Toward the end of Jesus' ministry on earth, two of his disciples took Jesus aside and made a play for power. These brothers, James and John, requested the seats of power to his right and left when Jesus would become king. They had no idea what they were asking. If Jesus had granted their request, they would have been crucified with him a few short days later. They didn't realize it then, but this was a pivotal moment, not just for James and John but also for the history of leadership theory.

So Jesus called the apostles together for an earth-shattering revelation:

> You know that those who are considered rulers of the Gentiles lord it over them, and their great ones exercise authority over them. But it shall not be so among you. But whoever would be great among you must be your servant. (Mark 10:42–43)

This was the first exhortation to servant leadership in human history. Up to that point, leaders demanded to be served. There was *no* expectation they would be the ones serving others.

Jesus makes an insightful observation. The phrase "those who are considered rulers of the Gentiles" could more literally be translated as "those who *promote themselves* as rulers." True enough, the crowds accepted their assessment and submitted to their demands. But it is the rulers themselves who crave to be seen as leaders.

Who are these "rulers of the Gentiles" Jesus speaks about? In Mark's Gospel, there are only two rulers appointed by the Gentiles: King Herod and Pilate. Against his will, Pilate executed Jesus, succumbing to the crowd's demands. Likewise, Herod beheaded John the Baptist based on a prideful promise to give his stepdaughter a prize for a lewd dance. In both instances, each man did what he didn't want to do in order to preserve his own image as a leader. *They were ruled by their desire to be seen as rulers.* They went against an inviolable law of leadership.

The only way out of this inevitable slavery to people's opinions is through servant leadership. That's why Jesus gave us this counterintuitive exhortation: "Whoever would be first among you must be slave of all. For even the Son of Man came not to be served but to serve, and to give his life as a ransom for many" (Mark 10:44–45). This was the first revelation of servant leadership *in all of human history.* Jesus started it. Had it not been for Jesus, there never would have been "civil servant" or "prime minister" roles created to serve the people. I want you to hear from Jeff some practical coaching about how you can become a servant leader like Jesus.

How Do I Become a Servant Leader?

Leadership, in a word, is influence. To influence someone is to move them in a new direction they are not sure about or simply don't want to go toward. We can accomplish this in one of two ways. We can either use our positional power to demand our teams move in a certain direction, or we can influence them by embodying the practice of servant leadership.

The concept of servanthood is tough for many leaders. They often mistake it for a "soft" trait that brands them as weak or even passive. But that perception couldn't be further from the truth. How do we most effectively influence people? By serving and supporting their ability to get results and be successful. As servant leaders, we don't focus on doing the work and getting the recognition for ourselves, but on ensuring our team is successful in what they need to accomplish.

When I first became a chief operating officer for a multi-billion-dollar international company, I had over 30,000 employees on my team. We were faced with low operating margins and client quality issues on dozens of accounts. There was no way I could be responsible for turning this situation around by directly digging in to fix the broken accounts. I made a decision to create a simple playbook through which my employees could develop operational excellence principles in their work.

Then, I got on an airplane and spent months traveling across the globe to serve our leaders by teaching them how to manage their work in a way that ensured successful outcomes. Within two years, our business had improved our operating margin by twofold, and quality was excellent.

Did I do the heavy lifting to make all these improvements? Of course not. The team did it. They deserve the accolades and recognition. I simply served them so they could be successful. Investing in the people we lead and removing the obstacles and roadblocks they face is the work of servant leaders. Simply put, our role is to empower, invest in, and enable people.

We need to make sure, as head coach of the team, that the players are at their very best and prepared to win the game. There are a few key questions to ask to help you assess your level of servant leadership:

1. *Do I believe in the team?* It's not about whether we like those on our team or if we think they are good, hard-working employees. The questions are: *Do I truly believe in them? Do I fully trust them? Do I not only believe in them to deliver on expectations and hit the objectives, but do I also believe in them when they fall short and make mistakes?* This is where the proverbial rubber meets the road with servant leadership: Are we willing to stand alongside our team in the good times and the bad? Will we counsel them, coach them, advise

them, and do everything we can to ensure they will learn from their mistakes and do better next time? As simple as this sounds, many of us forget what it was like to be new in a role, insecure with a decision, or lamenting a mistake we made. What we never forget, though, is how it feels to have a leader who verbalizes their belief in us and stands by us shoulder-to-shoulder, ensuring we learn and get better. Those moments stick with us for a long time and give us confidence and courage to continue to do well.

2. *Am I investing consistently in the team?* Are you making your team members a priority? Our greatest investment as leaders is our time and our experience. Sure, we can provide training and resources, but what people really need is our dedicated, undivided attention. They need to hear about our own lessons learned and the scar tissue we have accumulated on our journey. Our investment in the team is directly proportionate to the success of the team.

3. *Am I speaking straight and saying what needs to be said to the team?* Our teams need our honest and direct feedback. It is unkind to be unclear to those we lead. We may be tempted to sugarcoat tough feedback for fear of hurting people's feelings or causing them pain, or worse, for fear they won't like us. When we put others first, we must tell them what's needed for success. The reality is, we can serve our team best by providing them honest and direct feedback to make them better. Wouldn't it be crazy if you paid a personal trainer, and instead of the trainer speaking straight and telling you what you need to do to improve, they simply encouraged you and told you how great you are? You would fire them! Our team needs us to speak straight with them so they can be the very best in their roles.

One simple way to incorporate these attributes into your leadership style is to consider using a technique during one-on-one meetings with your team members called the "Triple A Method: Ask. Assess. Advise." Using this technique, you start your meeting by *asking* the team member how they're doing, which shows them you care about them as a person, first and foremost. It could be a question about their family, hobbies, or personal projects. It's important to show you care by acknowledging their value beyond their role as an employee. (Note: this must be authentic and not simply an exercise. This method lives and dies on personal connection and consistent investment.)

Second, *assess* how the project or objective is going by using clear, measurable feedback and data where possible, so that they know exactly how they are doing. Finally, *advise* them on how they might improve their results, remove roadblocks, or change their priorities to meet the deadlines.

This simple method of coaching your team is a great start to leading the team well by living out servant leadership. True servant leadership is not always easy; in fact, it may be the most difficult role you play in your own leadership journey.

Jesus, Son of Man

Jeff's advice above is not only helpful; it is biblical. God gave us more than pious platitudes in Scripture to teach us servant leadership. He gave us the model of his own Son. Jesus is the ultimate model, having made the ultimate sacrifice by giving his life for our redemption. Just so we're clear, this was not an accident. Long before his arrest, Jesus knew that he would willingly lay down his life. Months before it all unfolded, he declared his destiny: "Even the Son of Man came not to be served but to serve" (Mark 10:45). Serving is Jesus' life purpose; it is shown in the title he took, which epitomized his deep commitment to humble sacrifice: "Son of Man." It is an extraordinary title and the epitome of servant leadership.

Jesus is the ultimate model of servant leadership.

In the previous chapter, we observed Jesus' identity expressed through the title "Son of *God*." Here we see the other side of the coin: "Son of *Man*." This title is mentioned in the Old Testament 107 times (ESV). Of these references, 94 are found in a single book—Ezekiel. This title was God's designation for his prophet—a reminder to Ezekiel that he was a mere mortal—warts, pimples, and all. The title is not exactly an insult, but not really a compliment either. The purpose of the title was to point out human frailty. Jesus willingly took this title to identify his willingness to be with us, among us, and for us. While the term can sometimes be endearing, it's never flattering, except for one use in the book of Daniel. The passage in Daniel is the outlier, and it is the foundation for Jesus' self-perception as the Son of Man. This is a clue to what Jesus was up to in the incarnation.

Daniel 7:13 portrays the Son of Man as an exalted individual. In this unique passage, Daniel has a vision of God gloriously exalted on his throne. Suddenly a divine figure appears. It is none other than the "Son of Man" appearing in God's presence. In a stunning power play, the figure sits at God's right hand:

> And to him was given dominion and glory and a kingdom,
> that all peoples, nations, and languages should serve him;
> his dominion is an everlasting dominion, which shall not
> pass away, and his kingdom one that shall not be destroyed.
> (Dan. 7:14)

This is quite the conundrum. *How can a mere mortal attain divine status?*

Moving from Daniel to the New Testament, there is yet another quandary. "Son of Man" shows up eighty-five times, *always* referring to Jesus. We find all but four "Son of Man" references in the Gospels, and they are *about* Jesus and *from* Jesus.

Let that sink in. It is as if only Jesus has the gall to call himself a mere mortal. *Only Jesus is the "Son of Man." Only Jesus calls himself the Son of Man—and he calls himself almost nothing else.* This is a big deal. If the term "Son of Man" is one of denigration, except in Daniel, where it implies unprecedented exaltation, how does that jive with Jesus? How can Jesus be the exalted Son of Man who humbles himself on the human plane?

That is precisely the point of the incarnation. It is the promise of the Old Testament that God would come to his people and change their destiny. It is the embryo of Jesus' eternal biography. It is the foundation of servant leadership. The one with prominence and power willingly laid down that authority so he could lift us up. Servant leadership is not, however, merely what Jesus did for us; it is also what he calls us to do for others.

When we humble ourselves, God exalts us. It is a hard-and-fast rule in Scripture: "One's pride will bring him low, but he who is lowly in spirit will obtain honor" (Prov. 29:23). "Whoever exalts himself will be humbled, and whoever humbles himself will be exalted" (Matt. 23:12). "Humble yourselves before the Lord, and he will exalt you" (James 4:10).

Throughout his life, Jesus embodied this spiritual law. He came precisely to serve, not to be served, ultimately laying down his life on a cross. Because of that sacrificial death, God raised him from the dead and inaugurated him at the ascension to sit on his throne in heaven. He is King of kings and Lord of lords. His exaltation was predicated on his servant role, as is ours.

Jesus came to serve, not to be served, laying down his life.

After Jesus' resurrection, no human limitations of the "Son of Man" apply anymore. After the Gospels, all four uses of the title portray Jesus as a divine figure, no longer subject to human frailty. In Acts 7:56, as Stephen lies close to death, he sees Jesus high and exalted, occupying the throne at God's right hand. Hebrews 2:6 presents Jesus as the perfect model human being. Revelation 1:13 and 14:14 paint Jesus with the features of God. There is no longer any human frailty. The Son of Man and the God of Creation are the same. God made good on his promise that the one who humbled himself would be exalted.

The question for me has been: *Do I believe it?* Oh, I believe that it worked for Jesus. God absolutely exalted him because of his humble service. *But will he do the same for me?* That's the question I've wrestled with, not philosophically but practically. *If I don't promote myself, who will?*

I can hear you screaming at me through the page, "God will!" Yeah, yeah, I know. But man, have I struggled believing that. That's why after I preach, I often ask for feedback (hoping, of course, to fish for a compliment). That's why, when I publish a book, I check the ratings on Amazon. That's why we count followers on social media or hits on a website. That's why we compare attendance, profit margins, and salaries. Servant leadership sounds good on paper, but it cuts close to the bone in reality. That's why a clear view of our Father's approval is so critical for us as we learn to master servant leadership. But there is something more.

As I mentioned earlier, the "rulers of the Gentiles" are ruled by their desire to be seen as rulers. We see it in presidents who will do anything for reelection. We see it in coaches who will lie, cheat, and bribe their way to a win. We see it in executives who will cut throats and corners to get to the corner office. Leaders of all stripes use power and position for self-promotion and self-protection. Yet that desire to rule is the prison that robs them of the freedom to lead. That's when leaders forfeit their integrity for a title.

As difficult as it is, servant leadership is not optional for a Master Leader. Jesus' incarnation is not just a gift to us; it is a leadership model for us. Jesus showed how the Son of God could serve and suffer as the Son of Man. If we want God to raise us up as leaders, we need to lower ourselves as servants. That is the only antidote to being enslaved to our desire to be seen as rulers.

Chapter Summary

Servanthood is the bedrock of leadership. That is not a new idea. It goes back to Jesus himself. He was the first to ever truly lead through serving, and he called us to imitate his model. This is difficult in the midst of people's praise or the power that comes with promotion. When we fix our identity on the Father's approval, however, we gain the confidence to serve, even suffer, as Jesus did. Then we are freed from the bondage of self-promotion or self-protection, acquiring the bandwidth to focus on the things that matter most to God. It is this freedom that empowers us to steward well what God has entrusted to us. We'll turn to stewardship in the next chapter.

TAKE ACTION ON SERVANTHOOD

It takes a confident leader to use power to serve rather than self-preserve. That's why chapter 1 is the starting point for all Master Leaders. Servant leadership is the natural outworking of our secure identity and integrity. We are God's children, approved and empowered by the Father. The more fully we receive our identity from the Father, the more freely we can serve his children. The following two tools will help you assess and build your emotional intelligence toward service as a foundation for leadership development.

Leadership Self-Assessment

Measure Your Potential for Narcissism

After decades of research and mountains of literature, we know that the core advice of outstanding leadership has more to do with self-leadership than with leading others. This exercise provides twenty-three questions for you to answer using a Likert scale (1–5) for a self-evaluation that will help you measure how much or how little you are leading out of self-protection versus self-promotion. There are suggested follow-up exercises based on your score to move you more toward servant leadership. Download this exercise at TheMasterLeader.com/tools. Here's a sample of the type of questions you'll see:

1 = Strongly Disagree; 2 = Disagree;
3 = Neutral; 4 = Agree; 5 = Strongly Agree

Observation	Rating
I use "I/me" more than "we/us" when describing achievements.	
When faced with a tough decision, my primary concern is how it will impact my reputation or career advancement.	
I make decisions that primarily benefit me, even if they are not in the group's best interest.	

Take the full assessment when you download it at TheMasterLeader.com/Tools.

EQ Monitor

Build Self-Awareness and Emotional Tenacity

Leaders who lack confidence in their identity are prone to exercise authority for self-promotion or self-preservation. To grow in this area, check out the book *Emotional Intelligence 2.0* by Travis Bradberry and Jean Greaves. It can quickly help you make substantial strides in emotional intelligence; it was life-changing for me. To get you started in this area, however, I've designed three exercises you can complete this week to help you self-diagnose your emotional intelligence.

EQ Exercise #1: Agitation Triggers. Pull out the notes app on your smartphone and create a new note entitled "Triggers." For the next week, diligently track each time you feel agitated. Note:

- The specific date and time
- The person who triggered it (an anonymous driver, your spouse, a team member, etcetera)

- Their specific action (what they did or said, how they acted or responded)
- Your specific emotion (for example: frustration, anger, belittled, insulted, helpless, ignored, disrespected, mistreated, or judged)
- What you feel they "stole" from you

Once you have a list of ten situations, take it to three separate confidants. Ask them individually why they think these things upset you. Their outside perspective will likely give you insights into your emotional intelligence.

EQ Exercise #2: Talking Tally. Choose three conversations with three individuals from different spheres of your life (work, home, friends, relatives, etcetera). Without the individuals knowing what you're doing, keep a tally of how much time you spend talking compared to how much time you spend listening. Practice the art of getting others to talk more than you by asking questions that draw out their interests, experiences, and emotions. As a bonus, summarize what they told you in writing to hone your empathy and listening skills. The purpose of this exercise is simple: It is impossible to learn and talk simultaneously. It is also nearly impossible to show deference, respect, and interest in another person when you dominate the conversation.

EQ Exercise #3: Index Card Feedback. Pull out three blank index cards. On each, write three questions: What do I do that makes your job/life easier or harder? What are my potential blind spots? What practices would you suggest I work on to make me more effective at my job? Give these three index cards privately to three individuals you trust. Give one to a person "above" you (a coach, mentor, teacher, or supervisor). Give another to a peer (a coworker, friend, or family member). Give the third to someone "below" you (a student, employee, or client). Ask them for honest and private feedback.

3

STEWARDSHIP

Michael Lewis's 2003 book, *Moneyball: The Art of Winning an Unfair Game,* is a case study of how the strategic allocation of resources can give an organization an outsized advantage over the competition. Turned into a blockbuster movie in 2011, *Moneyball* follows the story of the Oakland A's Major League Baseball franchise. The club's budget was one-fourth of their competitors'. They simply couldn't compete in player recruitment. The team general manager at the time, Billy Beane, with the help of his front-office assistant, Paul DePodesta, adopted a radical new approach to player recruitment based on "sabermetrics"—empirical statistical analysis. Instead of prioritizing the usual statistics like batting averages, the A's employed this new strategy, looking at more undervalued metrics, such as on-base percentage (OBP) and slugging percentage (SLG).

They identified overlooked and undervalued players they could recruit for a dime on the dollar. Many had unconventional styles, perceived as weaknesses, but their statistical outputs didn't lie. Beane built a winning roster at a fraction of the cost. The results were remarkable. Despite losing three of their star players from the previous year and having one of the smallest budgets in baseball in the 2002 season, the team set an American League record with a twenty-game winning streak and a total of 103 wins, and they went to the playoffs. That success forever changed the way teams across several sports recruit players.

Moneyball captures how wise stewardship can empower you to do more with less. When we focus our resource allocation on things that give us the greatest gain on the field, we have an outsized advantage. While *Moneyball* is all about financial resources, the principle is equally true with our stewardship of time, talent, and words. Before I address Jesus' stewardship, let's listen to Jeff's counsel from a C-level perspective about how to steward resources well.

How Can I Steward My Resources Well?

As leaders, we feel the weight of responsibility to steward what God has put in our hands. With that accountability, we need to answer these questions: What have we done with what we have been given? Did we leave it better than we found it? If we had to do it all over again, would we use our resources in the same manner? Understanding stewardship really begins with understanding ownership. Who owns everything we have been called to steward?

As Christians, we know that answer is the Master. He owns it all. That means we have a responsibility to manage it well. We often think about stewardship in terms of financial resources, but stewardship is much more than money. It is also how we manage our time, our experiences, and our willingness to pour into our team.

1. *Time.* A key component of our stewardship as disciples of Jesus is how we manage our time. This requires us to think about our time both in and out of the workplace. "Work-life balance" is the term we usually use to describe how well we're balancing our work and our personal lives. For successful Master Leaders, balancing these two aspects of life is critical, and I find it helpful to think less about work-life balance and more about "work-life blending."

The reality is you will never find a *perfect* work-life balance. (I'm sure you know that already, but it helps to be reminded.) Whether we're in ministry or working in the marketplace, our work has heavy seasons that will require more time and energy than normal. Similarly, if you have a sick family member or you're experiencing a stressful season in your personal life, it may take most of your time to manage that.

The key is not perfect balance but rather the ability to blend the two dimensions of life—work and personal—in a way that serves both areas well. In my experience, I've learned that getting great at blending these worlds is more art than science. It's less about a formula or equation and more about an opportunistic attitude.

For example, it can mean taking a quick break during your busy workday to call home and check in on your spouse, or calling the hospital when heading into your next meeting to make sure your loved one is doing OK. Similarly, you may take advantage of a quick moment after the kids go to bed to give you time to respond to a few of the emails you weren't able to get to at work. The beauty of a well-painted masterpiece really comes down to how well the artist blends the colors and makes the background and the object feel like one unified picture.

I was in Germany on a two-week international business trip when I found out my daughter had won her cheer recital and moved to the regional championship—in the middle of my trip. My plan had been to save time by staying the weekend in Germany and then continue to India for the next week, since Germany was halfway there. After thinking about my commitment to not be an absent dad, I knew the right thing to do. I flew back to Phoenix, watched my daughter crush it at the cheer competition, and then got back on a plane and flew twenty-two hours to India. I met my commitment to both my daughter and my work. I put an extra 15,000 miles of wear and tear on my body, but I found a way to *blend* being a present dad and a committed leader.

This is what we need to do as Master Leaders. We need to be excellent at managing our time, talent, and treasures to accomplish being the very best we can be to all of our stakeholders at work, at home, and in our community.

2. *Experiences.* Stewarding our talent is about being open-handed with all that God has given us—including our skills, experiences,

insights, and lessons learned. As Master Leaders, we have an obligation to pass on what has been given to us. Information is power, and often leaders want to hold on to that power, choosing not to share it with others. But our heavenly Father calls us to a much higher purpose and never wants us to be a reservoir that holds on to what he has given us or allowed us to experience. Instead, he expects us to be like a river where resources and experiences flow through us to impact others.

Being a great steward means looking continuously for opportunities to share what we have with others; we must become a flowing river to the people God has entrusted to us.

3. *Pouring into our team.* I am currently mentoring three to four leaders at any given time, and although some would say that is too many and could be a distraction, I actually believe it is my role as a leader to continually pour into those who are hungry and want to learn and grow. Stewarding our experiences means we have to be willing to continually share and teach others what we have learned. Sometimes, it is as simple as providing quick feedback immediately following a presentation or after an interaction in a meeting. The point is to always be ready to share your perspective and feedback with your team, whether formal or informal.

Jesus' Stewardship of People

With these thoughts from Jeff in mind, we want to examine Jesus' stewardship. We will examine how Jesus stewarded the people God put under his care—his most important resource. We also want to consider how Jesus stewarded his words as a means of projecting his message. And finally, we'll look at how he ordered us to steward resources.

Throughout his ministry, Jesus was constantly bombarded with people. The crowds drove his preaching. Their sickness propelled his healing. Their antagonism caused his death. All told, Jesus had eighty-three individual encounters with people, as documented in the chart below (categorized by the type of people and topic of conversation).

Jesus' Interactions with People

Type of People	Topic of Conversation	Citations
Friends	Trust	Matt. 16:5–12; Luke 24:13–35; John 20:19–22
	Money	Luke 12:13–14, 32–34
	Following	Matt. 26:33–40, 73–75; 28:18–20; Luke 5:4–10; 10:1–2, 17–21; 11:1–13; John 6:26–69; 21:6–24
	Kingdom	Mark 9:35–37; 11:12–25; Luke 7:20–28
	Compassion	Mark 2:13–17; 6:34–44; John 11:17–27
	Cross	Matt. 16:21–25; 26:21–25; Mark 10:35–45; John 13:1–5
	Jesus' Identity	Matt. 3:13–17; 14:25–31; 16:13–18; 26:26–29; Mark 4:37–41; Luke 7:20–28; 9:28–35; 24:13–35; John 1:35–51; 11:17–27; 20:19–22
Seekers	Trust	Matt. 15:22–28; John 4:46–52
	Money	Matt. 19:16–23
	Following	Matt. 19:16–23; John 6:29–69
	Kingdom	John 3:1–6
	Jesus' Identity	Mark 11:7–11; John 19:17–19
Antagonists	Trust	John 7:2–5
	Following	Matt. 8:19–22
	Kingdom	Mark 3:21–35; Luke 5:33–39
	Sabbath/Rituals	Matt. 12:1–8; Mark 1:21–28; 3:1–6; 7:1–15; Luke 13:10–17
	Cross	Matt. 23:1–12; Luke 14:7–11
	Compassion	Matt. 19:3–9; Mark 5:1–20; Luke 4:16–30; 10:25–37

Antagonists	Jesus' Identity	Matt. 4:1–11; 22:15–46; Mark 14:55–65; Luke 2:46–49; 4:16–30; 13:31–33; 22:47–53; 23:7–12; John 2:3–8; 7:14–15, 37–39; 8:12–59; 10:10–14, 24–30; 18:28–31; 19:1–6
Outcasts	Trust	Matt. 15:22–28; Luke 7:1–10, 37–50
	Money	Mark 12:41–44
	Following	Luke 10:38–42
	Compassion	Luke 7:11–16; 15:1–32; 19:1–10; John 8:3–7
	Sabbath/Rituals	Luke 13:10–17
	Cross	John 12:1–8
	Jesus' Identity	Mark 5:22–43; John 4:10–14; 20:14–18
The Sick	Trust	Mark 2:1–12; 3:1–6; 9:17–24; 10:46–52; John 9:1–7
	Sabbath/Rituals	Luke 13:10–17; John 5:1–15
	Compassion	Luke 5:12–14; 17:12–19
	Jesus' Identity	Mark 1:30–34; 2:1–12; John 5:1–15

By looking at this chart, we can see how Jesus met people at their place of need, whether for healing, teaching, or confrontation. Whether friend or foe, he treated people with dignity, he spoke to them individually, he believed in their potential, and he called them to action and faith. Why? Because he saw people as a resource to be managed for God's glory, not his own promotion or protection. What is really surprising is that virtually all of these interactions were actually interruptions.

Virtually every interaction Jesus had outside of the Twelve was an interruption. A woman weasels through the crowd to touch him. A man bursts into the house to ask him to heal his son. A leper lunges toward him, pleading for healing. On it goes—dinner invitations, public confrontations, requests for healing, questions, and interrogations. If you think about it, most of our interactions are interruptions as well. We can view them as potential intrusions or potential investments.[4]

All leaders have an invisible influence account. We generally make deposits into others' lives slowly by habitual and consistent competence. Withdrawals, however, are made swiftly (often at a ratio of ten-to-one to deposits). *The best way to make leadership deposits more swiftly is through the appropriate management of interruptions.* A conversation at the grocery store, an emergency counseling appointment, an unexpected funeral, or a sudden sickness: these moments can magnify your influence not only with the recipient but also with those who hear the positive gossip. Interruptions, like crises, are pregnant opportunities for gaining influence.

What hinders our interruption influence is an overpacked schedule. If I'm honest, this is a weakness I'm working on. I can get so wrapped up in a project that, when someone pops into my office, it takes me two to three minutes to adjust my mind from the screen to their face. I have to constantly reinforce in my mind the importance of people over projects. One life hack that I've practiced poorly is to schedule thirty minutes, three times a week, to walk through office spaces for no reason but to hear what my colleagues are working on and to celebrate their wins.

Jesus' Stewardship of Words

Master Leaders are clear communicators. That was certainly true for Jesus. His messages were memorable, clever, and visionary. While there's much to learn about presenting formal messages (Andy Stanley and Lane Jones's book *Communicating for a Change* and John Maxwell's *Everyone Communicates, Few Connect* are two strong resources), we are concerned with something more visceral here.

How do you communicate on the fly to individuals or groups when circumstances avail themselves? In his book *You Lost Me*, David Kinnaman reminds us that "leaders rise and fall by the language they use."[5] What we say can have reverberating impacts, so we must be prepared to communicate well. Here is a short list of proven communication habits with the shortest fuse for effectiveness.

1. *Tell more stories.* We are wired for story. That's why Jesus used stories so frequently. By my count, the Gospels record thirty-seven different parables of Jesus. He knew that stories are the native language of communication. Recently, I was giving a training talk to our residents. Their glossy gaze indicated I had lost them. How could I get them back? Simple (I've used this frequently throughout my teaching career): "It's time for an irrelevant story." And just like Lazarus, they were back from the dead. In both formal communication and daily conversation, telling stories makes you and your words more memorable. They make you more interesting and more influential.

2. *Ask more questions.* Jesus was a typical rabbi who traded in questions. Even when he was asked a question, he often answered with a question. For example, when the chief priests asked Jesus, "By what authority are you doing these things, and who gave you this authority?" Jesus replied, "I also will ask you one question, and if you tell me the answer, then I also will tell you by what authority I do these things. The baptism of John, from where did it come? From heaven or from man?" (Matt. 21:23–25). Since John was Jesus' predecessor, his authority was also Jesus' authority. Part of the genius of Jewish pedagogy was asking questions as a means of guiding the learner to come to their own conclusion. It works just as well today.

So why do most communicators find asking questions difficult? It may be because we think that when we walk into a room, we're expected to have all the answers, not ask all the questions. (OK, let's be honest. No one believes that about us, except us. But hey, it feels good to pretend.) A Master Leader, however, realizes that questions are the best way of pulling brilliance from your team and the *only* way you can learn from them.

3. *Start with the audience.* It is entirely possible and irritatingly common for a communicator to be simultaneously interesting and irrelevant. Why is that? Because leaders often begin with their own agenda, interests, and experience. The goal of communication

is transformation, not information. That's why it is so important to start with the audience.

This principle is transferable to every conversation you have. If your assistant comes into your office, it may feel like an interruption. But if you start with their concern, they will ultimately be more effective. If you come home to your spouse and think through the day *they* have had, your conversation can start with their perspective rather than yours. This kind of empathetic respect can be powerful. The quickest route to personal significance is making others feel significant in their own personal setting.

4. *Repeat the vision.* Jesus was a broken record. On side A, he kept skipping at the same spot: identity—here's who I am. On side B, he kept repeating his vision: the kingdom of God. As leaders, we must keep repeating the vision and mission. When we marinate in the vision and mission every moment, we often feel like we are overcommunicating. But that is almost never the case. Repeat the vision until it is the choral refrain of the entire organization.

Jesus' Call to Steward Resources

Jesus had more to say about money than about heaven or hell. One could argue that his emphasis on money was due to his recognition that how we allocate our resources is a major indicator of our spiritual direction. Perhaps Jesus' theology of resource allocation is best summarized in his words in Luke 12:48: "Everyone to whom much was given, of him much will be required, and from him to whom they entrusted much, they will demand the more." According to Jesus, we are not owners; we are stewards. That's why we don't spend money; we *invest* it.

Organizations routinely and tragically miss their best investment opportunities by making the simplistic mistake of *static resource allocation*. Budget items tend to stay static year over year. Once a department or project is funded, the assumption is it will likely receive the same funding in perpetuity. You can look at your own organizational (or family) budget and see how, year over year, the percentages in each budget category remain relatively fixed although the technology, needs, and tools have changed. For example, how many years did your parents keep a home phone after they got a cell phone? Each year, we should be reevaluating every category in our budget to determine if it 1) is still needed, 2) has a positive ROI, and 3) still aligns with the vision and mission. If we could increase the fluidity of our budgets, we could more easily shift resources away from ineffective projects and people to those who are giving the team or organization the most benefits and creating the most momentum.

Each year, we should reevaluate whether our budget aligns with our mission.

Another tragic mistake of resource allocation comes when most organizations (and families) have no margin. They spend to the limit of their income. But without margin, you can never maximize the opportunities that require capital. By operating on 80 percent (or less) of your income, you can invest in dime-on-the-dollar opportunities. Yes, safe bets are best to build on. But occasionally, we must risk big, swing hard, and go long. Some call this "saving for a rainy day." Wrong mindset. It is investing in a dream yet to materialize. This "dream account" should be a line item in your annual budget. It creates the margin for the unexpected exponential investment.

Chapter Summary

Stewardship is the obligation of resource allocation—time, experiences, people, words, and tangible assets—that generates the most gains on the playing field. Many leaders believe they need more money or more talented people to make greater gains. This is seldom the case. Urgency and clarity are more valuable than abundance. Through shrewd resource allocation, we can do more with less than we ever imagined. The single resource we most need to manage is ourselves. The habits we create and the consistency with which we lead are of inestimable value to those we serve. But that is a conversation for the next chapter.

TAKE ACTION ON STEWARDSHIP

Stewardship is fundamental to leadership. By engaging with the following two exercises, you are taking a significant step toward mastering the art of resource allocation and energy management. These are not just tasks; they are opportunities to reflect, strategize, and innovate in your leadership practice. The commitment to complete these exercises is a commitment to your growth and the enhanced effectiveness of your organization. These action steps will help increase your impact in stewarding people, communications, and material resources.

Allocation Audit

Gauge How You Invest Resources

To invest resources wisely, *begin with the end in mind.* This is Habit #2 in Steven Covey's masterful book *The 7 Habits of Highly Effective People.* For any project, event, or task, ask: What is the "win" here for our church or organization? The answer will, of course, align with your mission and vision. With that clearly in place, wisely evaluate how you've allocated your resources.

Step #1: Account for your offerings (products or services). The organization we work with is a church, so we offer four services at Christ's Church of the Valley: the weekend experience, group ministry, students and kids ministry, and sports ministry. Those are the major ones. Our church also has food and coffee services on campus, digital training resources, website information, and a social media presence. In addition, there are some special events such as a daddy-daughter dance, camps, special needs events, weddings, funerals, etcetera.

Once you have listed your offerings, rank each one according to their alignment and effectiveness for carrying out the mission of your church or organization.

Step #2: Account for the percentages you invest in each offering. This includes tangible assets, people, time, and intellectual capital.

Give each major offering a specific percentage to do an audit of how many resources you give to each one. The numbers may surprise you, which is why Step #3 is important.

Step #3: Identify opportunities for resource reallocation. This might include moving a person from one department to another or creating a new task force to explore a new opportunity. It could mean thinning a team or reducing a budget, or perhaps releasing an individual from their duties to explore a new system or product. Because this type of reallocation is rare in most organizations, any economic shift you make will create discomfort until this becomes the new norm (which, in reality, could take years). That means it will be particularly important to persistently, perpetually, and convincingly "start with why," to quote the title of Simon Sinek's masterful book. If the mission is front and center, the people committed to the mission will adjust to changing resource allocation.

Energy Analysis

Diagnose and Strategize Your Energy Output

The Energy Analysis is a tool designed to optimize your personal efficiency. It will help you arrange your week in a consistently sustainable way. By systematically aligning your to-do list with your energy levels, you are taking control of your most valuable resource: time. This is not just about doing more; it's about doing what's right, at the right time, in the right way. This simple exercise may release your best creativity and consistency. Through it, you will not only boost your own leadership capacity but also set a powerful example of self-awareness and self-care for your team to follow. Download this exercise at TheMasterLeader.com/tools and complete it before moving on to the next chapter.

The Energy Analysis and the Allocation Audit are stepping stones to becoming a leader who not only manages resources and time effectively but also inspires and empowers those around them. Embrace them, learn from them, and let them guide you to becoming a Master Leader.

4

CONSISTENCY

Lance Armstrong won the Tour de France a record seven times. This alone would make him one of the greatest athletes in human history. He was a legend. Then add to that the fact that he accomplished this feat after beating cancer. However in 2012, the U.S. Anti-Doping Agency found Armstrong guilty of using performance-enhancing drugs. He was stripped of his titles and banned for life from competitive cycling.

Elizabeth Holmes, founder of Theranos, a medical tech company, was once hailed as the youngest female self-made billionaire. But in 2015, the *Wall Street Journal* exposed her fraudulent claims, and her company's lab was shut down. Theranos dissolved in 2018, and Ms. Holmes was indicted for fraud.

Ted Haggard was a nationally known pastor and president of the National Association of Evangelicals. He was a leading voice opposing same-sex marriage, until 2006, when allegations came to light that he had been engaged in misconduct with a male escort, compounded by drug use. Haggard's downfall destroyed his leadership legacy.

Bill Cosby, once celebrated as "America's Dad" for his role in *The Cosby Show*, faced numerous allegations of sexual assault spanning several decades. In 2018, Cosby was convicted of three counts of aggravated indecent assault. He ruined his reputation as a pioneering African American comedian and a moral voice for family values.

The most difficult leadership challenge is leading yourself. Whether in sports, business, religion, or entertainment, a lifetime of public success can be destroyed by private indiscretions. A Master Leader sustains trust through consistent private habits that build character over time. Jeff has some practical experience to share with us about how to build such habits.

How Do I Build Habits That Grow My Character?

Healthy teams require us to be able to rely on one another, to know we can count on one another through thick and thin, and to create that reliability requires us as leaders to be consistent in how we lead. Leadership consistency creates a sense of security for our teams, a North Star if you will.

As leaders, we know we must exercise many important transactional habits to be successful, such as goal setting, time management, and meeting efficiency. Much has been written on these habits, but I'm focusing on three key habits that aren't often talked about in today's leadership material. These are a few habits we think are key to being dependable, consistent leaders: decision-making, follow-through, and feedback:

1. *Decision-making.* Consistent leaders make clear and concise decisions. We make dozens of decisions each day. As leaders we have people watching and waiting for each decision so that they can take subsequent action. If we are unable to make clear and concise decisions, we risk paralyzing our team (and bottlenecking the project) as they wait for direction and clarity to avoid rework or the risk of moving in the wrong direction.

When I first became a CEO, I used to struggle with my team reacting too quickly any time I stated an opinion or view on a certain subject. I thought I was just brainstorming with them or helping them process out loud, but I came to find out they were hanging on tightly to every word I said. As Master Leaders, we must remember that our team has immense respect for us. They want to do great in their roles, and that means they are actively listening to not just what we say but how we say it. We need to be very clear when we are simply giving our opinion versus making a decision.

2. *Follow-through.* For some of us, follow-through is as natural as breathing air. For others, like me, it requires intentionality and accountability to ensure it happens. Look, no leader is great at everything. We can compensate for our weaknesses by relying on systems, processes, and technology as scaffolding for areas that don't come naturally for us. Notifications, alerts, and assistants can ensure we follow through on our commitments and keep the trust we worked so hard to earn.

If we make a decision and don't execute accordingly, our team can quickly lose confidence in us as leaders. They may perceive it as an issue of integrity when, in fact, it's often just forgetfulness or bad follow-through. We truly need to strive for a zero-gap approach to follow-through. If for some reason the decision or commitment needs to change, we need to be diligent and circle back with the team, letting them know both the change in direction and the "why" behind the change. Even though as leaders we are expected to be visionary, constantly looking at the future, if we don't follow through on yesterday's decision, we will create confusion and chaos for our team.

3. *Feedback.* The other habit that creates consistency is the ability to be direct at giving and receiving feedback. Not surprisingly, just like follow-through, speaking straight to others is a habit that's easy for some, but difficult for most leaders. The key to giving and receiving feedback is letting our teams know that, when needed, we will give them honest, meaningful feedback. As hard as it may be to make a habit of giving consistent feedback, it's important that our team knows that they're not wandering aimlessly—that they can count on us to give them the necessary feedback to help them stay on course and be successful in their role or project. The more we exercise

our courage muscle, the stronger it gets, and the more consistent we will be at providing meaningful feedback.

Whether we are leading in the marketplace or in ministry, learning how to say what needs to be said is an attribute that will serve us well throughout our leadership journey.

I was fortunate to begin my career at a large Fortune 100 company that made speaking straight a survival tactic, not a luxury. If you didn't get good at speaking straight in the feedback you gave to others and in receiving direct feedback, you quickly found yourself struggling and wondering if you would survive over the long haul.

As I transitioned into ministry from the corporate world, I found the situation to be quite different. Most people are filled with an abundance of grace and find it very difficult to speak straight with others. I believe we need honesty as much, if not more, in ministry. Jesus was very good at speaking straight, and he did it with love and grace. He set the example for us to do the same. Providing feedback is easier than receiving it. Both habits are required to be a Master Leader.

When you receive feedback, try this helpful hack: create space. Create enough space to allow yourself to *respond*—not react—to the feedback. We can immediately take a defensive posture to feedback and begin to justify or prove our rationale for our actions or position. Even the age-old idea of counting for a few seconds before speaking allows you to create space to give a more thoughtful response to feedback versus reacting out of emotion or defensiveness. When our teams know we will consistently and fairly give them feedback, and they can give us feedback that we will receive in a measured and consistent way, we provide a level of consistency that allows our teams to know they are heading in the right direction. We are there to make them successful.

Consistent character is always forged over time through the discipline of habits. As Jim Loehr and Tony Schwartz say, "Look at any part of your life in which you are consistently effective and you will find that certain habits help make that possible."[6] There is no magic wand to wave, no secret sauce. Character comes through the monotony of many small decisions stacked on each other. A leader's habits in the shadows ultimately evolve into character in the limelight. As the old adage says, "Your competency will take you only as far as your character will sustain you." Competency is seldom the leader's lid; character is.

Character comes through the monotony of many small decisions stacked on each other.

With Jeff's advice in mind, let's examine two of Jesus' most obvious habits to learn how to build our character. This is not to say that your habits must identically match Jesus' habits. But without character-forming habits, you will limit your leadership. We will begin with Jesus' most predominant habit.

Jesus' Habit of Prayer

The more popular Jesus got, the more he retreated in prayer: "Now even more the report about him went abroad, and great crowds gathered to hear him and to be healed of their infirmities. But he would withdraw to desolate places and pray" (Luke 5:15–16). Why did he retreat as his popularity grew? Because popularity, power, and fame are seductive. Jesus knew that. It seems that prayer was his defense against the onslaught of leadership influence. Without the consistent practice of prayer, few of us will survive the seduction of power.

We can draw three key insights from Jesus' well-documented prayer life:

Without consistent prayer, few of us will survive the seduction of power.

1. *Intimacy with God.* Topping the list is Jesus' unprecedented relationship with God. In every recorded prayer of Jesus, he addressed God as "Father." The only exception is the quote from the cross (Ps. 22:1): "My God, my God, why have you forsaken me?" His words show us the intimate

relationship of Father and Son. In a sense, this takes us back to our very first lesson on leadership—our leadership begins with our identity as God's children. Habitual prayer is a primary tool for building our identity.

2. *Major Events.* A second insight we can learn from Jesus' habit of prayer is his dependence on prayer before every major event of his life. He prayed before his baptism (Luke 3:21–22) and before feeding the 5,000 (Luke 9:16) as well as the 4,000 (Matt. 15:36). He prayed before walking on the water (Matt. 14:22) and preceding Peter's great confession (Luke 9:18). He prayed all night before choosing the Twelve (Luke 6:12). He prayed when he was transfigured (Luke 9:29), before raising Lazarus from the dead (John 11:41–42), and before instituting the Lord's Supper (Matt. 26:26–27). His most extended recorded prayer came before he went to the garden of Gethsemane (John 17), and he continued to pray in the garden before his arrest (Matt. 26:36–46). He prayed from the cross three times before his last breath (Luke 23:34; Matt. 27:46; Luke 23:46).

For Master Leaders, prayer should be our first response, not our last resort. Admittedly, I often find myself running to God only after I run out of options. But to truly imitate Jesus' prayer life and benefit from intimacy with the Father, our prayers must be as robust in the mundane as in the chaotic. If I were to be honest, this is my least-developed spiritual discipline, with the greatest potential upside. Because leaders master self-reliance and personal responsibility, prayer is a commonly neglected habit for leaders. We want to depend on ourselves rather than on the Father. But if we could learn to depend on God as we expect others to depend on us, our prayer lives could flourish. And Jesus provided us a model prayer to do just that.

3. *Modeling.* Jesus was so adept at prayer that his disciples asked him to teach them to pray (Luke 11:1). This model prayer, however, is not merely for us to get something out of God that we don't currently have. Instead, it may be the tool God uses to get something out of us that he currently doesn't have. With that in mind, what

benefits can Master Leaders derive from imitating Jesus' consistent prayer life?

A robust awareness of prayer's pragmatic advantages would motivate more leaders to come to God first. Prayer is a powerful tool for seeking God's counsel. It is a source to petition him for our needs. It empowers us to complete the mission God gave us. But you already know that, right? While all of these advantages should be sufficient motivation to practice prayer, in my experience, it is a radically underutilized resource for Christian leaders.

Jesus' Habit of Sabbath

Our greatest creativity doesn't come during activity. It comes in the margins. When I was a college professor, my creativity was shot in May at the end of a busy school year. After a couple of weeks of rest, however, I was able to write a half-dozen messages for the summer camps in just a few days. In my current role as teaching pastor, my day off is Friday. Saturday afternoon and Sunday are a marathon. If you were a fly on the wall in my home, you would be able to tell if I missed a day off. I'm less engaged with my bride and more irritated with traffic. Creativity, relationships, and triggers are not a bad barometer for how well we are doing with rest. This Sabbath principle is now widely accepted in secular leadership research. Jim Loehr and Tony Schwartz address workaholism as an addiction: "Unlike most addictions, workaholism is often admired, encouraged and materially well rewarded."[7]

The biblical principle of Sabbath states that we will achieve more in six days with God's rest than in seven without it. When we submit our days and dreams to God, it's as if we're placing them on the altar of his will. This weekly rhythm of consistent rest and worship marked Jesus' life. Luke writes: "And he came to Nazareth, where he had been brought up. *And as was his custom*, he went to the synagogue on the Sabbath day, and he stood up to read" (Luke 4:16). Jesus knew he needed the punctuation of rest and worship in his week.

It's interesting that Jesus ran afoul of the Pharisees more for "violating" the Sabbath regulations than anything else. Seven different times, he created controversy on the Sabbath (Matt. 12:1–8; Mark 3:1–6; Luke 13:10–21; 14:1–24; John 5:10–18; 7:21–24; 9:1–7). It wasn't that he neglected Sabbath rest. It was that he didn't submit to the Pharisees' onerous rules of *how* one should rest. The issue was important enough to fight about because, in Jesus' own words, "The Sabbath was made for man, not man for the Sabbath" (Mark 2:27).

The Power of Sabbath

Part of the power of Sabbath is it puts us in a position to manage the stress of the work God has called us to. I see this most clearly in how I handle criticism. Jesus' model, again, is incredibly insightful. He was criticized for all sorts of things: fraternizing with sinners (Mark 2:15; Luke 15:1–2; 19:1–10), not following proper protocol for ritual cleansing (Mark 7:1–23; Matt. 15:1–20), claiming to be divine (John 10:33), and being "demon-possessed" (Mark 3:21–22; John 10:19–20), as well as for threatening the temple, not paying taxes, sorcery, and allowing women to follow him. But more than anything else, he was criticized for not following Sabbath regulations.

I find this interesting because it was Jesus' life of prayer and practice of Sabbath that empowered him most to deal with criticism. The brutal truth is that there's no way leaders will avoid criticism. It just comes with the territory. But *how* we handle it can reveal to others the quality and consistency of our character.

Here are three practical steps to manage criticism in a way that cultivates consistency of your character—proven steps that work for me when I encounter criticism.

1. *Recognize that seldom is the issue the real issue.* People who criticize and complain often are dealing with unseen pain that you likely have nothing to do with. In my first ministry, there was a woman who called me like clockwork every other month just to cuss me out

for about thirty minutes. It was brutal on a young pastor. Around the third time, I called her back about a week after the incident and asked, "This seems to be a regular pattern. Am I really upsetting you regularly?" Her answer took my breath away. "Oh no," she admitted. "It's not really about you at all. I just have so much pain in my family, and sometimes I get so mad at God. But I can't kick him. So I take it out on you." Well . . . good to know!

2. *People tend to criticize what they don't understand.* When you explain the "why," many can adjust to the "what." Be careful here, though, because criticism often comes through email or social media. If we've learned anything over the last two decades, we've realized it's just impossible to diffuse dissent online. Nor do you need to. The revolving news cycle and the pubescent attention span of social media are your friends. Online sparks seldom turn into flames unless you fan them. Occasionally, they will take on a life of their own, but that's rare at the local level. Email is a slightly different story. Sage advice on responding to email is the three-sentence rule:

- Thank you for sharing your perspective.
- I have read your opinion and have taken it into consideration.
- We are grateful for your reaching out to try to make us better.

Do not defend—whatever you do. The more words you write, the more responses you'll receive. The cardinal rule is that email begets email. Unless you're willing to meet face-to-face, email warfare is toxic.

3. *The more a digitally delivered criticism triggers you, the longer you should wait to respond.* Twenty-four hours is the minimum gestation period for a response. If you realize you're triggered, take two or three days. If someone replies with a secondary email of complaint, it will sit in my inbox for a week—if it ever gets a response. There will be no third email. If you're wondering whether a delayed response will just push people away, the answer is yes, exactly. That's

the point. Your mission will grow by your consistently following a higher calling, not responding to a lower criticism.

> **Follow a higher calling instead of responding to a lower criticism.**

Balance and consistent rhythms of worship, rest, and work are essential for the consistent life that marks a Master Leader. When one area of our life is out of balance, it will impact the consistent habits in other areas of our life. Rest and worship are the fuel for spiritual and emotional health.

Our day should be punctuated with work, home, and sleep. Our week should be punctuated with work, rest, and worship. Our year should be punctuated with celebrations. The Jews call(ed) them festivals; we might call them "holidays." But the purpose is the same—devoted time to realigning the priorities of God and family above your work and career. With a biblical balance of rest and worship, we can work more productively.

Chapter Summary

Consistency is key to leadership longevity. That's why the boring habits in the shadows are so essential to ensuring and securing our public legacy. Private practices such as prayer and Sabbath sustain the consistency of our character over time. Most of us can be great in a moment; few of us can be consistently good over a lifetime. That's what differentiates good leaders from Master Leaders. If you're wondering how you're doing, how you handle criticism is a pretty good litmus test of the health of your habits. When you maintain your private disciplines, the public pressure of criticism is sustainable. The reason consistency is so critical is that without these "boring" habits, we will lack the bandwidth *to care* for our people. And that is really the heart of leadership, to which we turn in the next chapter.

TAKE ACTION ON CONSISTENCY

Master Leaders come in all shapes and sizes with various gifts, personalities, and propensities. However, the one constant is that we are all creatures of habit. Our habits, especially the boring ones, make us most effective: Making the bed each morning. Answering emails each day at a specified time. Writing thank you notes. Working out. These kinds of "boring" habits reduce decisions, minimize variables, and maximize strategies. The following exercises are designed as a starter kit for cultivating effective habits.

Consistency Metric

Weigh the Reliability of Your Habits

The Consistency Metric is a simple chart to help you track your consistency for two weeks across ten habits. What makes this so powerful is that each of these habits are what we call "cornerstone habits." These are practices that naturally replicate themselves in other daily practices. When you master any one of them, they "spill over" into multiple other areas of your life, making you exponentially more disciplined. Go to TheMasterLeader.com/tools to download the Consistency Metric to start cultivating your leadership efficiency.

Keystone Habits

Measure the Habits with the Highest ROI

The Keystone Habits exercise is a chart that lists eight primary habits that Craig Groeschel, founder of Life.Church, suggests as key habits for leaders. You can download the details and an explanation of this exercise, along with a simple chart at TheMasterLeader.com/tools. This three-step exercise will help you rank your habits, choose key habits to focus on, and improve on keystone habits over the next six months. Not only will this help you self-evaluate your key habits, but it will also help you build those that will offer the greatest immediate impact in your leadership. These practices are simple (not easy, but simple). Whether you are a novice who doesn't know where to start with habit formation or a veteran leader with plenty of scar tissue, these exercises will increase your consistency, and increased consistency multiplies your leadership exponentially.

5

CARING

While 2020 will be remembered for the novel coronavirus, it was also rife with leaders abusing people with their power through bullying and sexual misconduct. In 2020, Jerry Falwell Jr. fell from grace at the evangelical college Liberty University due to a series of sexual and financial allegations. He failed to live up to Liberty's ethical and moral values. In that same year, the famed apologist Ravi Zacharias lost credibility when multiple confirmed cases of sexual abuse surfaced *after his death*—proving that there is no statute of limitations on moral failure.

Sexual scandals ran the gamut of social institutions. In politics, former New York governor Andrew Cuomo resigned under the scrutiny of multiple sexual allegations directly in opposition to his publicly espoused values. Dan Snyder, former owner of the NFL team Washington Commanders, was accused of fostering institutional sexism in the organization. Even earlier, in 2016, sexual scandal plagued Michigan State University as hundreds of female athletes accused Larry Nassar, the team doctor, of sexual misconduct. He violated one of the most sacred vows of the medical profession. And actor Kevin Spacey, in 2017, watched his "house of cards" fall as he faced multiple allegations of sexual misconduct, spotlighting the #MeToo movement's influence in the entertainment industry.

Again in 2020, quite apart from sexual or financial scandals, talk show host Ellen DeGeneres faced accusations of fostering a toxic workplace through bullying. A year later, the identical accusation was made against nationally known church leader and author Mark Driscoll in the popular podcast *The Rise and Fall of Mars Hill*. DeGeneres and Driscoll could not be more opposite socially, yet both shared the accusation of using their platform and abusing their power to mistreat those they led.

The accusation all these leaders shared in common was not caring for the people God entrusted to them. When leaders abuse their power for personal gain, we are naturally aghast. Jesus, in stark contrast, used his power exclusively for the powerless. Rather than using power for self-promotion or self-protection, he used it to care for those who needed it most. That truth has become the vanguard of servant leadership. Love was Jesus' primary value. But before we look at how the Gospels address this, I want you to hear Jeff address the importance of a point leader caring for his people.

How Do I Care for Those I Lead?

Most leaders understand the principle that no one cares how much we know; they want to know how much we care. I recently read author and psychologist Henry Cloud's book *Trust*. In it, he identifies and unpacks five key areas necessary to create trust. The first pillar he talks about is understanding. He says that for someone to trust you, they need to know you understand them, that you have taken the time to listen and care for them.[8] Care is a staple for trust, and trust is essential for leadership. People follow leaders who care. Trust is one of the most critical ingredients to a healthy relationship.

The organization we lead will live or die on the level of trust we create as leaders. For our team to trust our leadership, we must become leaders our team can count on to live out our values and actions. Transparency and vulnerability are two key fundamentals we need to build trust. Let's take a look at these fundamentals:

1. *Transparency*. This relational fundamental can be scary. Often, situations that require transparency are difficult. For example,

sometimes we need transparency to deliver bad news. Other times, we need it to talk straight with our team. And still other times, we need transparency to admit when we are wrong and take responsibility. In most instances, transparency will ultimately build trust with those we lead. Let me be clear: transparency doesn't mean we share all things with all people; rather, it means we use discernment to share the important things at the appropriate time to ensure our team is aware of key information they need to be successful in their roles.

Transparency often includes giving the people on your team a sneak peek or heads up about important information yet to be shared with others. Consistent transparency is an action that can be critical to ensuring a team member is properly prepared for an upcoming change or an issue that may affect the team or organization. As leaders, we owe it to the people we lead to be transparent and minimize the amount of surprises we put on our teams. No one likes being caught off-guard. Because transparency is not a muscle we exercise consistently, it's important to get into a routine of making it a sustained habit we implement often.

2. *Vulnerability.* If we think transparency is a bit uncomfortable, the habit of vulnerability is really going to feel awkward, especially if you don't currently practice it. No doubt, vulnerability feels risky for leaders, but it also can be extremely powerful. Vulnerability says to our team, "I'm willing to take a risk with you. I trust you." When we are willing to be vulnerable with others, we show our humanness as well as our believability. Consistent vulnerability is not only a key element of creating trust; it's also contagious.

When we lead by example with vulnerability, we give our team permission to do the same. Obviously, vulnerability requires us to set limits and exercise discernment. I encourage you to share only appropriate emotions, struggles, and personal stories and to never cross inappropriate boundaries that may put your working relationship at risk. But my guess is that most of us are not in jeopardy of being overly vulnerable. Instead, we stay safe and risk very little.

In chapter 1 we talked about blind spots. These are excellent places to cultivate the habit of vulnerability. If we take risks, become real, and consistently show our team who we really are as a leader, we will exercise vulnerability. I know for me this area of vulnerability has paid great dividends as I have learned to exercise it more and more throughout the years. Surprisingly, it has paid the greatest dividends in the highest leadership positions I have held.

I remember standing in front of my extended leadership team, a room of about twenty-five leaders, and sharing with them the importance of listening and how we communicate with clients. I shared an example of when my wife confronted me about my harsh tone, even though she agreed with what I was trying to say. I let the leaders in the room know how easy it is to fall into this situation. At the next break, one of my vice presidents approached me and said, "How do you do that?"

"Do what?" I asked.

"Share shortcomings with all of us in the room."

I chuckled and realized it had become so common for me to use personal examples to show my own shortcomings and vulnerabilities that I didn't even realize I was doing it. It had become second nature. Trust was built on the spot.

In ministry, the concept of care is straightforward—we are pastors, so we care for people. But in the marketplace, the concept of caring for your team can sometimes come across as soft. After all, we need to get results, make things happen, and achieve our sales goals. I've served in both arenas, and I'm telling you that the leadership principle of caring for your team is not just biblical—it is smart! If we know that our emphasis is on achieving results, it only makes sense that, as leaders, we would focus on what gets results. Trusting and caring for our people gets results!

So why is it that we often neglect to care for the people who make the results happen? Think about athletes and how teams get results. In Major League Baseball, if a starting pitcher makes 100 or more pitches in a game, he will take four to five days rest before he pitches again. Does Major League Baseball do this to win an award for "kindness to their players" or "best place to work"? Of course not. They're smart. These teams want to win games, and they understand the way you win games is to have healthy athletes that are in the best possible condition. Take a lesson from Major League Baseball and make caring for your team a priority. Our care for people is expressed through our consistency and is part of our stewardship. Such care requires serving people, which is, of course, dependent on our developing integrity. These Master Leader characteristics are mutually interdependent.

Jesus' Primary Value: Love

With Jeff's coaching in mind, we now turn to how Jesus cared for people in all kinds of ways. He healed, taught, defended, confronted, and ultimately died for the people he cared for. The foundation of his care was his primary value of love. We can find its highest expression in the familiar verse John 3:16: "For God so loved the world, that he gave his only Son, that whoever believes in him should not perish but have eternal life." Twice in Jesus' life, he encountered the perplexing question, "What is the most important command?" Let's look at Mark 12:28: "One of the scribes came up and heard them disputing with one another, and seeing that he [that is, Jesus] answered them well, asked him, 'Which commandment is the most important of all?'"

On the surface, that question might seem difficult. After all, the Jewish Bible had 613 recorded commands, not including the myriad of oral traditions, which were held with nearly equal weight to the Scriptures. However, there was one command that towered above the rest. It comes from Deuteronomy 6:4–6 and is called the *Shema* (named after the first Hebrew word in the verse), meaning

"Listen!" This command was so famous that it has been recited in every synagogue service from then until now. And it continues to be a daily Jewish prayer, rolled in little scrolls and tucked into phylacteries (those little boxes worn by rabbis on their foreheads and left arms) and the *mezuzahs* hung on doorframes of Jewish homes.

What is this important command? The answer was obvious. In fact, we heard this very question a year earlier in Jesus' life. During Jesus' itinerant preaching tour, a lawyer approached him—not a lawyer like we're used to today, but an expert in the Mosaic legislation. He asked a question designed to trip up Jesus: "Teacher, what shall I do to inherit eternal life?" Jesus' response was brilliant. He let the lawyer answer his own question, knowing that most lawyers would rather talk than listen. Jesus asked, "What is written in the Law? How do *you* read it?" The lawyer took the bait. His answer was a conflation of Deuteronomy 6:5 and Leviticus 19:18: "You shall love the Lord your God with all your heart and with all your soul and with all your strength and with all your mind, and your neighbor as yourself" (Luke 10:26–27).

Notice that the lawyer's answer in Luke 10 is identical to the answer Jesus would give during his final visit to Jerusalem: "'Hear, O Israel: The Lord our God, the Lord is one. And you shall love the Lord your God with all your heart and with all your soul and with all your mind and with all your strength.' The second is this: 'You shall love your neighbor as yourself.' There is no other commandment greater than these" (Mark 12:29–31).

Both scenarios identify the two great commands: to love God and to love our neighbor. The reason the second command is always connected to the first is simple: you can hardly love God without caring for your neighbor. After all, we can't climb a stairway to heaven to give God a hug or mail him a care package. Our love for God can only be enacted through our care for our neighbor. Because God loved us, we are commanded, above all else, to love him. Deuteronomy 6:5 is as famous among Jewish people as John 3:16 is among Christians. According to Jesus, this command cannot stand alone. It is paired with Leviticus 19:18: "You shall love your neighbor as yourself."

Jesus is right, of course. These are not two separate commands. You cannot love God except by caring for your neighbor. Oh, if love were a feeling, you could. One could worship at church, pray in private, burn incense in a temple, or any number of other expressions of adoration. However, Christian love is an outward orientation of practical, sacrificial action, not an internal emotion of affection. So how can we treat God with sacrificial love? He doesn't need anything from us pragmatically. You can hardly feed him, clothe him, or provide medical assistance. How can we express our love for God practically? Every parent knows the answer: "You show love for me when you care for my kids." Treating someone's children with kindness is the highest expression of love. To that end, Jesus enjoined us to love two broad categories of people.

Christian love is outward, sacrificial action, not internal affection.

"Love your neighbor." At first, this command might sound simple. People around us often share our economic level, cultural values, and common interests of safety and socialization. For Jesus, however, "neighbor" was defined differently. When the lawyer approached Jesus in Luke 10 to ask him how to inherit eternal life, the end of this discussion was a simple command: love your neighbor. However, the lawyer, wanting to justify himself, asks Jesus for clarification: "Who is my neighbor?"

Jesus' answer is both brilliant and overwhelming. He told the story we now know as the parable of the good Samaritan. Note: the phrase "good Samaritan" is never found in the Bible text. The Jews hated Samaritans (people from Samaria); that's the punch of the story. By the end of the story, which is likely familiar to you, Jesus changed the question in two ways. First, the lawyer used a specific word for neighbor, meaning "those living *near* me." He could've used another word which meant "those living *around* me." So it seems that the lawyer is already trying to truncate the category of neighbor and limit it to those in close proximity. We might expect Jesus to object to the narrower definition of neighbor. He does not! Instead, he allows the narrow definition, even limiting it to your arm's length. However, according to Jesus' story, your arms go wherever you go. So your neighbor becomes anyone you can touch, and it includes everywhere you go!

Jesus makes a second change to the lawyer's question by turning the question on its head. The lawyer asked, "Who is my neighbor?" By the end of the story, Jesus asked, "Who was neighborly?" For the lawyer, "neighbor" was a noun. But for Jesus, "neighboring" is a verb! Eternal life, according to this parable, is not about being in the company of the religious elite. Eternal life is about acting on behalf of those in need.

This story was so compelling that it transformed Western culture. Because of the contagious nature of this idea, our society seeks to help those in need. The United States, for example, is the only nation in history that rebuilt the enemies we destroyed after World War II. As a culture, we designate special parking places for those with disabilities. We offer special protection to refugees and the poor, and billions of dollars go into peacekeeping efforts for other nations. This is not to suggest that we are a Christian nation or that Western society honors Jesus in every way. It is to assert, however, that many of the noble attributes of our modern Western world are directly linked to Jesus' value of caring for our neighbor.

This idea of "being neighborly" aligns with what Jesus said about loving our enemies (Matt. 5:44). In the Middle East—then, as well as now—loving your enemy is not theoretical theology. It is not "liking" terrorists or oppressors. It is practically and pragmatically caring for the needs of those who may threaten the welfare of your family. Nuts, right?! In Jesus' day, loving your enemy might have included housing a Roman soldier, feeding a Samaritan, clothing a thief, or harboring a refugee. There is simply no way to sugarcoat this or make it more easily digestible. And there is no way to explain it away as if we no longer have the responsibility to care for those who may do us harm.

There's no wiggle room to weasel out of this. Within two years of uttering these words, Jesus modeled loving *his* enemies who pinned him to a cross. Think about the first thing he said at his public execution: "Father, forgive them, for they know not what they do" (Luke 23:34). One who forgives his enemies in the middle of a crucifixion has the moral authority to ask us to do the same. As difficult as it was for Jesus to do, his selfless request on the cross paled in comparison to the sacrifice of the Father to offer his own Son to the disobedient and rebellious. That's *all of us,* not just the Jewish leaders and Roman executioners at Golgotha. We are all undeserving beneficiaries.

If we are to claim to be Jesus' followers or Master Leaders, then his value of loving God by loving others is of paramount importance to our agendas. Whether we're building a church, company, community, or family, caring for others is the hallmark of a well-lived life.

If we follow Jesus, then loving others tops our agenda.

Chapter Summary

"Care" may seem like such a mushy word for leaders, especially those type-A, hard-charging bulldogs. It is not! Our love for the people we lead is a far stronger motivation for action than selfish advancement. It is the purpose of all we do as Master Leaders. This principle of leading with love is a foundational constant of leadership. Everything else, however, changes. People's needs change, times change, and opportunities and challenges change. That's why Master Leaders must be nimble. How? Well, that will require a longer discussion, which we will tackle in the next chapter.

TAKE ACTION ON CARING

The values of your church or organization will drive the direction of it. This fact is irrefutable. The question is whether the organizational values printed on the wall actually *live* in the hall. Do your church/organization's lived values align with Jesus' values? I'm not saying your values must be identical to Jesus' or expressed with similar verbiage (although "caring for people" is a non-negotiable). But anything that drives us that's not ultimately driven by love will inevitably be less effective and less enduring, whether we lead a church, a company, a restaurant, or a school.

Clarifying organizational values in behavioral terms is critical to providing guidelines and guardrails for team behaviors. To that end, here are two practical action steps you can take to help you identify and implement organizational values built on how we care for the people we lead.

Engagement Guide

Care for People by Becoming a Life-Giving Leader

If people are our greatest resource, then stewarding them is our highest priority. The good news is it's easy to do in our current cultural context. The following three simple actions can make you the most popular person on the planet.

Exercise #1: Greet people like a long-lost friend. Practice raising your voice, posture, and excitement in the first three seconds of a greeting. When you see someone, stand up, extend your hand, and exclaim excitedly, "Ryan, so great to see you. Man, my day just got better!" Scheduling an extra five minutes before and after each meeting to engage someone in this way will earn you a great deal of influence with minimal investment of time. Be the kind of person that people are excited to see because you are excited to see them.

Exercise #2: Learn about their family. Studies have shown that there is nothing more powerful than the sound of a person's name. Make a note on your phone called "People." Create categories based on where you interact with people: church, office, neighbors, gym, clients, customers, etcetera. Then write down the names of people you interact with in these places (assistants, committee members, colleagues, etcetera). Add the names of all their family members (this is, of course, an ongoing list). If you forget someone's name, make it a practice to say, "I'm so sorry, I'm embarrassed, but I forgot your name, and my ego is less important to me than knowing your name, so could you please tell me your name again?" They will be happy to tell you their name. They will feel valued and will appreciate your transparency.

Exercise #3: Engage in their interests. Walk through the office and notice the items people have on their desks (pictures, sports memorabilia, hobbies, and clues for favorite restaurants and vacations). Find a way to ask about one of those items. It could be as simple as, "Man, what a game last night!" or, "I saw on Facebook that your son won the tournament. You must be so proud." In whatever ways you can, celebrate the wins and mourn the losses of their life. You will build loyalty by showing you care for people where they are.

Values Workshop

Identify, Wordsmith, and Advertise Your Values

Gather your key leaders for a daylong retreat and spend some time identifying the gap between your perceived values and your actual values. As a team, list your values (use a whiteboard, if possible). You should land somewhere between five and eight values. Now, sharpen these to a laser focus. Once you have that ranked list, it's time to wordsmith your values and make them "sticky." Think in terms of a bumper sticker, not a tweet. Your initial list should strive for exacting clarity. Reshape and rework the wording until it's memorable, even impossibly unforgettable. The goal here is that these sayings become slogans across your organization. When a visitor comes and asks about your organization, everyone from the senior pastor or CEO to the back-row consumers should be able to spit out the same slogans.

Here is an example from Christ's Church of the Valley in Phoenix, where Jeff and I serve. Our values form an acrostic:

Commitment to excellence
Heart for evangelism
Relationships
Integrity
Servant attitude
Team over talent

Now it's time to advertise and reward. The advertisement is the easy part. Print your values on posters, post them on your website's home page, and give them exposure through promotional materials or messaging. Say them over and over in staff meetings until they become part of your staff's verbal DNA.

This will only happen, however, if you move from PR to HR. You can't just *talk* about internalizing your values. You must reward it. People repeat what you reward. This could be through "Culture Awards" or gamification of values (competition, point scoring, rules of play), but ultimately, advancement in the organization should be tied to promoting your values-based culture as much as it's tied to productivity. Promotions, bonuses, and public recognition will create and replicate the culture that's rewarded.

If you lead an organization, your personal proficiency becomes an organizational deficiency if *you* are out of alignment with the values of the organization. For example, a church leader may champion noble and successful ministries that, in reality, distract and drain the church's energy from its primary mission. A business leader might introduce a product line out of alignment with the company's goals.

We are only as good as our team. Remember, the team trumps talent every time. This is why the Master Leader is crystal clear on the organization's values. If you have had success in another organization but seem to be bumping up against a brick wall in your current organization, this is an area to investigate. It's one of the hidden roadblocks of success for the most competent and creative leaders.

6

NIMBLENESS

Remember Kodak? The brand was the uncontested giant of the photography world. Founded in 1888, they had nearly a century of success owning both the camera and film industry. They even created the first digital camera in the 1970s but failed to recognize this new technology as the future of photography. Instead, they clung tenaciously to their film cameras because that was their principal cash cow. As a result, competitors outpaced them in the digital space, leading to their ultimate bankruptcy in 2012. Their refusal to change strategy turned out to be devastating.

Blockbuster was once the premier brick-and-mortar behemoth for movie and video game rentals. At its zenith in the 1990s, its blue-and-yellow logo sprawled across the country. The fledgling mail-order service of Netflix, struggling to become profitable, offered to sell to Blockbuster. The behemoth refused, ultimately signaling their demise. While Netflix adapted to customers' preferences and began streaming, Blockbuster held firm to late fees and physical storefronts. They closed their final stores in 2014.

What both of these stories teach us is that strategy must be nimble. Just so we are clear, the mission, vision, values, and culture of our church or organization are firmly fixed. Strategy and stewardship, however, must be flexible. How we carry out the mission will morph with opportunities, challenges, and shifting culture. Operational flexibility is imperative to the success of the mission. New situations demand new methods; new opportunities require reallocation of resources. To put it colloquially, "Marry your mission, but date your strategy."

This is counterintuitive for most leaders. Why? Because what worked in the past holds emotive memories: "It was this worship style that grew the church." "It was the door-to-door sales approach that built the company." "It was a particular brand of rhetoric or social stance that put a pastor on the map." Our memories can be resilient when attached to our emotions. That's why Master Leaders must cling tenaciously to the mission but be nimble with the strategy. Jeff has leadership scar tissue in this area. Hear his perspective on how to stay nimble without losing focus.

How Will I Stay Nimble While Maintaining Focus?

Strategies and objectives for a church or an organization are like the game plan or playbook for a sports team. Your mission is to win championships. The strategies you incorporate and the plays you run are how you will make the win a reality. While many coaches often try to fit their players into the designed playbook, one could argue that the playbook should be adjusted to fit the players they have on their roster. Author and nationally recognized Pastor Craig Groeschel asserts, "Most leaders are trying to figure out the right strategy. The best leaders are obsessed with empowering the right people."[9] In other words, the best leaders focus on the right players more than the right plays.

Even the best thought-out plans often fail to achieve the outcome we intended. Why is that? Is it because our strategy was misguided or our objectives were not well-written? Or is it more likely because we didn't have the right people on the project or in the right role? Maybe we had all the right people on the bus, but we didn't have them in the correct seats. Possibly any of those scenarios could be true, but it might be another subtlety that leaders often miss. That subtlety is the ability to be adaptable and nimble. We often miss the opportunity to be flexible because we fall in love with our strategies, objectives, and plans.

In my experience, most leaders have developed really good strategies and plans. The challenge isn't the quality of our plans but rather the fact that our world is constantly changing, and the context that made perfect sense a few months ago may be all but out the window today. This is why, in today's world, it is so critical that we spend less time trying to develop a perfect plan and spend more time developing the skills to be nimble and to manage change effectively. Disruption is not a question of "if," but rather "when" and how severely the disruption will impact your well-laid plans.

Need I say more than the great disruptor, COVID-19? It wasn't just what COVID did to rock our world; it was how well, or not so well, we responded to it. Many companies, as well as churches, in the United States found themselves paralyzed and unable to discern the next step, so they just froze. How organizations responded to COVID and its impact made all the difference, and ultimately determined whether they are now thriving organizations and churches or just surviving—or worse, no longer even around.

Look, for another example, at the great NFL coaches with the winningest records. Believe it or not, their winning records are not due to having the very best strategies or game plans. They are due to their ability to assess how the game is progressing and what they need to do to adjust their game plan to win the game. Great coaches don't fall in love with their game plan. They take a few minutes at halftime to go into the locker room and confer with the other coaches, study the first half of play, and make personnel and play adjustments, and then they go back in the second half looking very different than they did the first half.

You often hear broadcasters say, "This is a whole different team in the second half." If you think about it, wouldn't it be crazy if the coach had a horrible first half, simply lamented with the team at halftime, and then said, "Go out and do the exact same thing in the second half as we did in the first half, and let's see if we can win this game"? That coach wouldn't have to worry about their next season; their successor would.

As leaders, we need to recognize that the power that nimbleness brings to an organization is the difference between success and failure. Rarely do we ever win with our original strategy. For example, when I was CEO of a startup company, the board of directors and I were confident we had a go-to-market model that would be the talk of the healthcare industry. However, our strategy was trying to fix a problem the healthcare executives did not have. Our plan was well-intentioned but did not position our product to meet our clients' needs. We had two choices: change the model and grow, or stay with our original strategy and lose valuable momentum, time, and resources. We made the decision to pivot our strategy and change our model.

Nimbleness is our ability to adjust to new realities and make the needed changes. The heart of nimbleness ties back to humility. If we fall in love with our ideas and plans, we will never consider changing them because we think they are perfect (or because we fear that people will find out *we* are not perfect). Humility allows us as leaders to be able to say, "I thought I had a solid plan, but things have changed, and if we don't change our approach, we will be in a world of hurt."

That level of humility will serve us well as Master Leaders and will set the table for nimbleness and flexibility. Remember, it's not how we *start* as leaders; it's how we *finish*. As the apostle Paul reminds us, we press onward toward the prize. In other words, forget about the first half; make the needed adjustments and press on toward the second half to have the best chance to be successful. Master Leaders don't necessarily need to be the smartest leaders with the best plans. We just need to be leaders who are willing to make the necessary adjustments to ensure a successful outcome.

Shepherd: An Ancient Model for Nimble Leaders

Jeff's advice is spot-on. And the Bible uses the metaphor of a shepherd to help us adopt and adapt this kind of nimbleness in our own leadership context. Shepherds had to be agile for their flocks to survive. Perhaps that's part of the reason the shepherd was the primary model of leadership in the Bible. A quick survey of shepherds in the Bible might reveal a thing or two about how to lead with agility.

All shepherding in the Bible begins with the Good Shepherd in Psalm 23. Jesus, the Lord, made the same claim in John 10. Shepherding was a metaphor for Jewish leaders in Ezekiel 34 as well as for elders of the church in Acts 20. The most famous shepherd, of course, was the author of Psalm 23, King David. His time in the field was his best preparation for the throne: "He chose David his servant and took him from the sheepfolds; from following the nursing ewes he brought him to shepherd Jacob his people, Israel his inheritance. With upright heart he shepherded them and guided them with his skillful hand" (Ps. 78:70–72).

The same could be said for Moses. It was his forty years in the wilderness with Jethro's flocks that prepared Moses for his forty years of leading Israel through the desert. Before Moses, there was Abraham (Gen. 13:5; Exod. 3:1; Ps. 77:20; Isa. 63:11). He passed on the family business to Isaac, who passed it on to Jacob (Gen. 29–31), who married a shepherdess named Rebecca (Gen. 29:9). Virtually all the heroes of the faith were shepherds in the field.

This is where Master Leadership begins: doing for our flock what God has already done for us. When God delegates his authority to kings, priests, and prophets, he expects them to lead like shepherds. For Yahweh, "shepherd" is no mere metaphor; it is a strategy. We use our power for protecting the sheep, not self-promotion. Our rod and staff are for guiding the sheep. We lead the sheep so they can feed and rest by quiet waters. It is a peculiarity of Middle Eastern shepherds that they lead sheep. In the rest of the world, sheep are primarily driven.

How does leading sheep relate to being a nimble leader? A nimble leader is one who is able to quickly adjust to changing situations, without losing focus on the primary goal. Take David, for example. When he first stepped into the national spotlight, he came from the flocks to the battlefront (1 Sam. 17:15, 20) and found himself face-to-face with a giant warrior. King Saul encouraged him to wear his armor. But it didn't fit the young shepherd. Instead, he chose the nimble accouterments of his own experience rather than the bulky armor of others. Rather than allowing his peers to pressure him into their expectations, he kept focus on the goal: kill the giant. He had faced lethal opposition before in the form of a lion and a bear (1 Sam. 17:34). His agility with a sling catapulted him to success (1 Sam. 17:40).

The heroes of the faith all applied their agility in the field to the obligations of their leadership. Shepherds had to be flexible. They were *constantly moving* from one pasture to another looking for the most fertile food for their flocks. Weather, geography, and bandits required constant vigilance to assess both threats and opportunities. Shepherds also had to carefully, even meticulously, *monitor the health* of the flock. Of all the flock animals, sheep are the most susceptible to disease, predators, parasites, infections, and the just plain stupidity of wandering off. Only a nimble shepherd could adjust to the ever-altering needs of sheep. Their watchful eye, quick decisions, and bold confrontation would protect and move the flock.

Nimbleness is needed for leaders today—for many of the same reasons shepherds needed it. In the Middle East, shepherds didn't typically own the land their flocks grazed on. They were allowed to move through farmers' fields (adding fertilizer along the way). Because shepherds provided a valuable service—providing meat—they were valued. But they were also suspect. Their constant movement through other's areas opened them up to accusations.

Anything that went missing could be blamed on itinerant shepherds. (Are there any leaders out there who have been falsely accused?) Because shepherds were strangers (and lonely), they caught sexual liaisons where they could. Anonymity has never bolstered morality. (Any lonely leaders out there who have been tempted to shortcut morality to assuage the pain of your position?) As an occupational hazard, shepherds were physically dirty. More than that, they were ritually unclean since they constantly slaughtered animals, bred sheep, and delivered lambs. The needs of the sheep, the ever-present predators, and the accusations of the community required shepherds to be nimble. Can anyone out there relate?

The only constant in leadership is change, except for one thing: the flock. We lead the flock, feed the flock, and protect the flock. Always. Those leaders who lost focus on the flock got a brusque rebuke in the Bible. We find the most brutal reprimand in Ezekiel 34. It's a full-throttle, frontal assault on the rulers of Israel who fleeced the flock rather than feeding them: "You eat the fat, you clothe yourselves with the wool, you slaughter the fat ones, but you do not feed the sheep. The weak you have not strengthened, the sick you have not healed, the injured you have not bound up, the strayed you have not brought back, the lost you have not sought, and with force and harshness you have ruled them" (Ezek. 34:3–4).

Any of us who take up the mantle of leadership should consider this warning well: *God will hold leaders responsible for the well-being of the flock.* Shepherds who sacrifice sheep for their own benefit rather than laying down their lives for the sake of the flock will answer to the Chief Shepherd over the flock. The lack of self-sacrifice is perhaps the biggest barrier to being a nimble leader. Change isn't just difficult for followers; it's often difficult for leaders. It is more comfortable to sit in a pasture and play the lyre than to move the sheep.

God will hold leaders responsible for the well-being of the flock.

"Nimble" and "sacrificial" are often synonymous. We see that, of course, in Jesus' shepherding strategy. He wasn't just flexible; he was sacrificial. At one point, he and the boys needed some R & R. They tried to escape to the opposite shore of the Sea of Galilee. But the clamoring crowds raced nine miles around the lake to find them. When Jesus disembarked, he ran headlong into a throng numbering 5,000 households. His response showed sacrificial agility. He saw the people as "sheep without a shepherd" (Matt. 9:36).

Jesus adjusted his plans to meet the needs of the flock. Virtually all of his personal conversations and miracles were initially interruptions. He adroitly altered his agenda to maximize the opportunities to shepherd the flock in front of him. And when one went astray, he went after them. In fact, only twice did Jesus repeat a parable, and one of those instances was about leaving the ninety-nine sheep in a field to go find the lost one.

Nimble leaders know that plans change but the primary agenda never does. The paths we take will vary constantly. The hurdles we overcome, the threats we face, the healing we provide—they're all driven by the circumstances we face. But the flock is the constant North Star for Master Leaders.

Chapter Summary

Changing times require nimble leaders. We all agree with that, at least in theory. The challenge comes with actual change, which is often most uncomfortable for the leader. It requires effort in learning new skills and humility to adjust to the needs of our people. As leaders, are we willing *to change direction to lead, feed, and heal the sheep?*

These are the primary characteristics of a Master Leader: integrity, servanthood, stewardship, consistency, care, and nimbleness. Jesus modeled them for us as the original Master Leader. It is time now to turn our attention in Part 2 to specific actions that will flow from these characteristics. We will begin with building culture, which is at the root of our organizational practices.

TAKE ACTION ON NIMBLENESS

Nimbleness is a necessary characteristic of a Master Leader. In today's whirlwind world, the ability to lead through change is not just an add-on asset; it's essential for survival in leadership. The agility to adapt, pivot, and thrive amidst uncertainty will set you apart as a leader. These two tools will equip you to build a resilient team. Engaging with these exercises is the first step toward transforming challenges into opportunities and innovation in your organization. The first will help to build resilience in your team during change. The second is an easy way to identify potential areas for change.

Change Management

Create an Action Plan for Change

Identify what needs to change now:

- Prioritize changes: It would be unwise to change too much too quickly. Assess what needs to change in the next three months, the next year, and the next five years.
- Engage key stakeholders: Involve church elders, ministry leaders, influential members, or other key stakeholders in affirming these priorities for change and in executing these changes. The broader your buy-in, the more landmines you will avoid and the less resistance you will encounter.
- Set realistic goals: Establish clear, achievable objectives for each change initiative.

Advice for communication:

- Transparent messaging: Clearly communicate the reasons for the changes and how they align with the church's or

organization's vision. Express why before how and why more often than how.
- Regular updates: Keep the congregation or your team informed about progress and setbacks in a consistent manner. Remember, you live with this every day. When you think you have overcommunicated, double it, and then you *might* be close to communicating enough.
- Encourage feedback: Create avenues for members or constituents to voice their concerns. Prioritize face-to-face communication with leaders rather than email. This gives you the chance to reiterate the "why." Articulate that you are listening, not that their complaints will change the plan.

Dangers to watch out for:

- Resistance to change: Be prepared for some resistance and have a plan to address it compassionately. Again, you are not changing direction but listening compassionately.
- Overcommitment: Avoid trying to implement too many changes at once, which can lead to burnout or cause your "ministry account" to go into the red.
- Guard the culture: Ensure that changes respect and integrate with the existing church or organizational culture. Guard the respect for the past as well as the vision for the future.

Tips for mental health:

- Personal time management: Balance your workload with personal time to avoid burnout. You might want to revisit the Energy Analysis from chapter 3.
- Spiritual health: Maintain your own spiritual practices to stay grounded and focused. Be sure you are surrounding yourself with life-giving people.
- Seek support: Don't hesitate to consult with mentors, counselors, or peers when feeling overwhelmed.

Tracking the team's emotional adjustment:

- Regular check-ins: Initiate frequent, informal conversations with team members about how they're handling the changes. They need to be aligned with and support the talking points of the point leader.
- Observation: Pay attention to shifts in morale, engagement, and participation among the team. Watch for extroverts who become more silent. Monitor absenteeism or those arriving late or leaving early. Your artists and creatives can be your best allies or your most invective opponents. Be sure to affirm them during change.
- Provide support resources: Offer workshops, counseling, or group discussions to help team members navigate through the change emotionally.

Secret Shopper

Get Outside Input on Your Values

Sometimes we are too close to see the changes we need to make. It's the old "crack in the windshield" syndrome. We stop seeing what is so obvious to others. One quick solution is to find someone in the community who is unfamiliar with or unaligned with your church or organization. Invite them (or even hire/incentivize them) to "mystery shop" your services.

If it's a church, ask them to attend a worship service. If it's a business, ask them to engage as a customer. After their visit, ask them what impacted them positively or negatively (or both). What would they change if they were the point leader of the organization?

The most important things to change most quickly are those that are out of alignment with your values. If your mystery shopper cannot pick up on your values, then likely the values you think you have are not the values you and your team consistently live out. Various employees (or volunteers) will have different personalities, varying maturity levels, and various skills. Nonetheless, your values—when clear and rewarded—will be reflected regardless of the individual differences in the people you lead.

PART 2

THE ACTIONS OF A MASTER LEADER

In Part 1, we focused on the six leadership principles necessary for developing the *character* of a Master Leader. Now that we have learned how to assess and prioritize the very fiber of what it takes to be a Master Leader, in Part 2 we'll focus on six specific *actions* of a Master Leader. These are the practices that best build our teams. It starts with *building culture* and *casting vision*. Once these are in place, we move to *developing strategies* and *focusing our priorities*. Finally, we address *taking action* and how to ultimately leave a legacy by *mentoring future leaders*. These practices, modeled by Jesus, will separate you from the mass of marginal leaders. Jesus is not only our Master; he is a masterful leader. Following that leader will make you a Master Leader as well.

7

BUILD CULTURE

As Peter Drucker, the legendary father of modern management, famously says, "Culture eats strategy for breakfast—all day, every day." That's why Master Leaders work hard on the culture of their churches or organizations. Culture is not created through plaques on a wall or inspirational speeches but rather through specific behaviors that are allowed, promoted, or rewarded (or all three). And most of all, culture is created by the actions a leader models. In my research for this book, I ran across a few positive (and somewhat surprising) examples of how successful organizations have created culture through specific behaviors.

The Ritz-Carlton Hotel Company values exceptional customer service. That's why they empower every employee to spend up to $2,000 to address any guest issue. By giving employees the authority to address customer concerns immediately, they can provide on-the-spot resolutions to prioritize guest satisfaction.

Southwest Airlines values a corporate culture of fun. They encourage flight attendants to create their own script to infuse humor and personality into in-flight announcements. Some flight attendants are practically stand-up comics, and the passengers who just herded themselves into their seats sometimes applaud their efforts.

Google values innovation. Therefore, leaders allow employees to use 20 percent of their work time on personal projects outside their primary role. This provides mental margin for innovation and cross-pollination of other departments. This practice directly contributed to some of their most valued products, such as Gmail and Google News.

The Container Store (my wife's mecca) values employee development and well-being. They provide extensive training for new employees, often more than 260 hours. That's why their knowledgeable workforce can offer superior service and advice and point you to organizers you never knew existed.

Patagonia (which is far more my jam than the Container Store) values environmental responsibility. Their Worn Wear program provides repair guides and services and also sells used Patagonia products. The program models a commitment to sustainability that counters the fast-consumption cycle standard in the fashion industry.

Each of these organizations not only states its values on its website but also integrates specific behaviors into its operations, training, and rewards systems to live out those values. They don't let culture happen; they cultivate it. As James Clear says in his classic book *Atomic Habits*, "Goals are good for setting a direction, but systems are best for making progress."[10] Personally, I don't know of anyone more expert at creating organizational culture than Jeff. I've asked him to coach us on how to do that.

How Do I Create a Strong Culture?

Healthy leadership cultures often exhibit a key behavior that I believe should be the example, *not* the exception: the key behavior of personally living out the values of the culture they're creating. A universal principle of leadership is that you can never take someone further than you have gone yourself. Think about the Sherpas that Mount Everest climbers hire to take them to the summit. They want someone who has traveled those paths many times in all kinds of weather and has found the best routes to take. Can you imagine employing a guide who has never experienced the journey you are about to take? It would simply be the blind leading the blind. Well, that's precisely what happens when we ask those we lead to do as we say and not as we do.

For example, I was part of an executive team where the stated expectations were for us as leaders to be consistent and not show favoritism. However, one of our top leaders would consistently give special roles to close friends and have them not report through the normal organizational structure but directly to him. This happened with three or four positions, until finally, I approached him and let him know these exceptions were creating distractions across the leadership team. The leader understood the issue and agreed to eliminate the reporting exceptions.

As leaders, we need to earn the right to be heard, and we need to create culture by putting in the time and effort to live out what we are asking our team to do. Master Leaders say, "I won't ask you to do something I'm not willing to do myself." Our teams are willing to take the field for us as long as we are willing to walk side by side with them on the journey. The key is for us to be leaders who live out the values we say matter most to us.

Culture, in any organization, is not about a set of high-flying values espoused by the leaders at the top. Rather, culture is a collection of behaviors an organization exhibits day in and day out—actions specifically demonstrated by the organization's top leaders. Many of us have been part of organizations where the values say one thing but the organization operates very differently in practice. Being a leader by example means we translate the values of the organization into the actions and practices that help implement those values into daily life.

I believe that one of the best ways we can lead by example is by living out the behaviors that best represent the values we claim to uphold as core beliefs. Conversely, the quickest way we can create culture erosion in our organizations is by creating exceptions to the values and policies we put in place. Exceptions are the dangerous antidote to a healthy, sustainable culture. They absolutely devastate the trust our teams have in our leadership. It is the epitome of "Do as I say, not as I do." Unfortunately, the exceptions we make can scream louder than the 99 percent of the time we live out the right cultural behaviors.

There are many examples of this, but one that has really stayed with me over the years was a very senior executive in our organization who talked in town halls and public meetings about the importance of teamwork and trust. Whenever a certain company leader was absent from a meeting, the senior executive would immediately begin to criticize him. This executive had the top seat in the organizational chart and was large and in charge, yet due to his great insecurities he made it a point to make fun of and point out flaws in this other leader whenever possible. I remember the sick feeling in my stomach as I watched this behavior for years.

I watched the culture of that executive team degrade month by month as a spirit of fear, intimidation, and lack of trust began to permeate all corners of the organization. Eventually, the criticized leader left after many years of service and went on to be successful leading a large company. Unfortunately, I watched many other executives follow the senior executive's lead and make it a habit to put down leaders who intimidated them or whom they simply didn't like. Since this behavior was happening at the very top of the organization, it spread like cancer, leaving a wake of damage in its path. When I left this organization and went to a company where trust and teamwork was lived out, my eyes were opened to a whole new world of what a healthy culture could look like.

We all have examples of what a healthy and an unhealthy culture looks like. The challenge is how we create that healthy culture. There are two key aspects to creating a healthy culture: 1) how specifically we define the behaviors we expect from the team and what it looks like, practically, when these behaviors are lived out, and 2) how we create a cadence, or ritual, of talking about these behaviors constantly throughout the work week.

Although this may, at first, appear boring or uninspiring, this is what makes culture simply how we "think, act, and execute." When you ask someone who works in a thriving culture to explain what's so great about their culture, they usually respond by saying, "I'm not really sure; it's just how we do things around here."

Culture is shaped by what we, as leaders, *reinforce*, *reward*, and—most importantly—*allow*. As James Clear says, "What is rewarded is repeated."[11] Of course, it's important to spend time focusing on what we reinforce and reward, but what our teams really take note of is what we allow. When bad behavior is allowed to take place, it is like a huge eraser that wipes out many of our efforts to reinforce and reward the desired behaviors—for example, allowing an unhealthy or even toxic leader to continue in their role, or having a double standard of making the lower-ranking staff follow a certain policy while allowing senior leaders to ignore it. What you allow speaks louder than you might think. Culture is not easy, but it is simple: define what you want it to look like, talk about it constantly, catch (and acknowledge) people in the act of living out the desired behaviors, and then be very careful about what you allow. Culture matters to Master Leaders!

With Jeff's expertise in mind, let's look at how Jesus created culture through two specific behaviors he modeled, promoted, and expected from his followers. Previously, we saw that his primary value was love. That value was practiced through two specific behaviors: *mercy* and *inclusion,* both foundational for creating a loving culture.

Jesus' Behavior Mandate #1: Have Mercy

For Jesus, the ideal of "love" came from the Hebrew word *chesed* (roughly translated "mercy"). *Chesed* speaks of God's loving mercy, based on covenant loyalty. It's thick with meaning. Jesus modeled this kind of mercy and seems to have been impacted by Hosea 6:6: "For I desire steadfast love [*chesed*] and not sacrifice, the knowledge of God rather than burnt offerings." This passage must have been pivotal for Jesus since he quoted it twice. One time was in Matthew 9:13, when the religious leaders accosted him for including Matthew, a tax collector, in his group. Jesus' retort was quick and sharp: "Go and learn what this means: 'I desire mercy, and not sacrifice.' For I came not to call the righteous, but sinners." The second time Jesus quoted these words from Hosea came in Matthew 12:7 as he defended his disciples for picking heads of grain on the Sabbath. He said, "And if you had known what this means, 'I desire mercy, and not sacrifice,' you would not have condemned the guiltless." Notice that, both times, Jesus was defending his disciples so they could be included in his entourage.

This brings up an important point. Mercy can be savage. It's not simply about being nice or showing compassion. Mercy has a ruthless bent to defend the oppressed. For example, the prophet Zechariah (speaking for God) demanded of the people, "Thus says the Lord of hosts, 'Render true judgments, show kindness [*chesed*] and mercy to one another'" (Zech. 7:9). Likewise, the prophet Micah said, "He has told you, O man, what is good; and what does the Lord require of you but to do justice, and to love kindness [*chesed*], and to walk humbly with your God?" (Mic. 6:8). Jesus, when he criticized the religious leaders of his day, said: "Woe to you, scribes and Pharisees, hypocrites! For you tithe mint and dill and cumin, and have neglected the weightier matters of the law: justice and mercy and faithfulness. These you ought to have done, without neglecting the others" (Matt. 23:23; see also Luke 11:42).

Jesus' followers kept catching him in the act. He perennially practiced mercy. Twice, two blind men pleaded for mercy, and Jesus healed them (Matt. 9:27; 20:30–31). On another occasion, a Canaanite woman pleaded for mercy for her demonized daughter (Matt. 15:22). Later, a father pleaded for his demonized son and likewise received God's mercy through Jesus' healing (Matt. 17:15). In Mark 5:19, a recently exorcized Gentile asked Jesus to allow him to join his entourage of followers. But Jesus declined with this instruction: "Go home to your friends and tell them how much the Lord has done for you, and how he has had mercy on you." And a band of ten lepers were granted the mercy of the cleansing they requested (Luke 17:13). Is it any wonder, then, that both Matthew and Luke record a similar beatitude from the lips of Jesus? "Be merciful, even as your Father is merciful" (Luke 6:36; Matt. 5:7).

Jesus' mercy features prominently throughout his ministry and is recorded in each of the Gospels. But there is something worth noting in these stories. Mercy was not merely an act of kindness Jesus did for others. It was how he built his group of followers. Chris Voss built his career as a negotiator practicing Jesus' principle. He observes, "[You] don't treat others the way you want to be treated; treat them the way you need to be treated."[12] Jesus taught this in loving our enemies and outsiders. Mercy was the mechanism for inclusion. It was then; it is now.

> **Mercy was how Jesus built his group of followers.**

Jesus' Behavior Mandate #2: Be Inclusive

Being inclusive in the kingdom of God is different than "inclusion" in our culture. We are not talking about approving another's lifestyle regardless of its alignment with God's expectations. Rather, Jesus-style inclusion centers on embracing people where they are to help walk them into God's plan for their life. To do that, the Master Leader must be centrifugal.

Let me explain. Jesus' teachings and actions demand an outward orientation. You can't follow his example without continually pushing the boundaries ever outward. Though most rabbis taught that the blessings of Abraham were meant for Israel, Jesus affirmed that the blessings were *through* Israel. His words tapped into prophecies like Isaiah 42:6: "I am the LORD; I have called you in righteousness;

I will take you by the hand and keep you; I will give you as a covenant for the people, a light for the nations."

Because of Jesus' centrifugal purpose, he promised that Gentiles would enter the kingdom, even those deemed enemies. Ninevites and the Queen of Sheba (Matt. 12:41–42; Luke 11:31–32); Sodom and Gomorrah (Matt. 10:15; Luke 10:12; Matt. 11:24); and Tyre and Sidon (Matt. 11:22; Luke 10:14)—they would all gain entrance into the kingdom. In fact, Jesus reversed the objects of judgment and reward so that Israel would be judged and Gentiles rewarded (e.g., Matt. 11:20–24; Luke 10:13–15; and Matt. 8:11–12; Luke 13:28–29). That went over like a hot dog at Hanukkah!

Although Jesus never openly reached out to the Gentiles, he set a trajectory through his ministry that made ethnic inclusion inevitable. One of the main ways he set the wheels in motion was through meals. Jesus ate with "sinners," not merely as an act of compassion, but as an invitation to repentance and a subsequent declaration of their acceptance into the kingdom of God. In fact, he was declaring "impure" people to be model citizens of the kingdom of God. It was not, apparently, that their impurity was ignored but that Jesus effectively "healed" sinners through his table fellowship as comprehensively as he did the sick by his touch. Luke 19:9 expresses this as clearly as any text: "Today salvation has come to this house, since he also is a son of Abraham."

Jesus' openness to "outsiders" became the vanguard of evangelism. Outsiders could become insiders. That is precisely the point of the Cornelius episode of Acts 10 (Acts 10:10–13; see also 11:3). Jesus' table fellowship turned the social tables of insiders and outsiders. That model of inclusion is desperately needed, not just for church leaders but also for business leaders. While state and federal laws prohibit discrimination in hiring practices, they make no mandate for table fellowship. Obviously, I am not merely suggesting we eat with employees (although this has huge upsides). I'm asking a pointed question: *Who is invited to your table? Who do you let into your inner circle?*

Confession: I grew up in a church that was "believe, behave, belong." You were not really part of the church until you believed the same things and conformed your lifestyle to the other members. For me, that meant such silly things as styles of music, clothes, movies, and language. So when new people came, they were clearly left out. In my ignorance (and I'm now desperately embarrassed about this), I looked down on men wearing earrings. (Don't judge me! It was the 1970s. Ugh.) I talked about love for the lost. But I couldn't love anyone well until they believed like me and looked like me. I've since changed—thank God! The church I now serve has a different mindset: belong, believe, behave. You are welcome to the table long before you align with our beliefs or behaviors. As a result, for the last ten years we have continued to grow by 10 percent year over year, baptizing more than 10 percent of attendees. It is extraordinary what inclusion does for creating culture.

For business leaders, this may have a different expression in your organization. But one thing is exactly the same: for Jesus, love needed a tangible expression. His value of love for people manifested in his behaviors of mercy for those who were near and inclusion of those who were far. For those of us who claim to love God, we have no option but to adopt practical behaviors that demonstrate love for God's children. The apostle John summarized it succinctly:

> **Jesus's culture of loving people manifested in his mercy and inclusion.**

> By this we know love, that he laid down his life for us, and we ought to lay down our lives for the brothers. But if anyone has the world's goods and sees his brother in need, yet closes his heart against him, how does God's love abide in him? Little children, let us not love in word or talk but in deed and in truth. (1 John 3:16–18)

Chapter Summary

Master Leaders create culture by clarifying, modeling, and rewarding specific behaviors that embody the values the organization espouses. Jesus' highest value was love. To create a culture among his disciples around that value, he practiced mercy and inclusion. That culture continued in the church they established—a church that was known for the inclusion of the rich and poor, slave and free, Jew and Gentile. His centrifugal mercy transformed prostitutes and tax collectors into apostles and evangelists.

Leaders don't just build organizations; they reconfigure culture. Ultimately, the culture the Master Leader wants to reconfigure extends well beyond the boundary of their own organization. We are not building a church or a business—we're building God's kingdom. But that is a conversation for the next chapter.

TAKE ACTION ON BUILDING CULTURE

To create a culture based on your values, every department and each individual must be clear on which behaviors model and implement the organization's values. This requires us to identify, clarify, promote, and reward behaviors that model the organizational values. Furthermore, behaviors that betray your values must be identified, clarified, and confronted. Remember, your culture will be determined by the behaviors you reward as well as those you allow. So how can leaders help their teams know the rules for engaging with others? Take action with these two exercises.

Behavior Matrix

Clarify Behavioral Standards to Create Your Culture

Master Leaders set the culture in their organizations by establishing rules for engagement that reflect their values. The number of stated values of the organization should not exceed seven. However, the behaviors to establish those values may be a couple dozen. How do you establish those behaviors?

Begin by bringing together a team of key leaders and creative thinkers. For smaller organizations, this might include key stakeholders and volunteers. Start by identifying the best performers in the organization—not just the most productive people. You want to look at who's most cohesive for the team. These individuals do their job with excellence and inspire, encourage, and train others to build teams.

List the specific actions these champions do that make them so valued by the team. Put the list next to your organizational values and identify how these specific behaviors model and promote your values. Then ask what other behaviors would be paramount for creating the culture you want. It's probably better to go crazy at this point. Build a thick list of forty or fifty behaviors. Then cut, combine, shift, and sift the list to between twelve and twenty-four behaviors. Next, wordsmith the list to make each item sticky. Here are a few examples from our organization:

"We are the example, not the exception."

"We create great experiences."

"We honor the absent."

Each value should be represented by two or three specific behaviors.

Behavior Modification

Promote and Reward Value-Creating Behaviors

Once you have your sticky list of behaviors, call an all-staff meeting to roll them out, even if your staff is small. Walk through each behavior, explaining why it's important to the organization's values and, ultimately, the culture. Offer concrete examples from specific people who exemplify that behavior. The more your people can visualize and personalize these behaviors, the quicker they will be able to adopt them and help create culture. No one individual will master them all, but all can master several. These behaviors, each championed by exceptional examples, become the working vocabulary of the organization, defining your culture.

The next step is to catch people behaving positively and reward their attitude and efforts. This could be as simple as a social media post or an all-staff email highlighting a difference-maker. This might be gamified through trophies, awards, and plaques. It could include financial compensation with a bonus, a raise, or a promotion. Whether people receive honor or an honorarium, these behaviors will expand in direct proportion to the recognition and reward they bring.

Conversely, when someone betrays the team's values, you will now have a vocabulary for confrontation. Ignoring bad behavior is a reward for the offender and an offense to the rest of the team. Silence debilitates the leader's ability to create a positive culture. Ignoring bad behavior is simply kicking the can of confrontation downhill, where it can pick up steam, allowing broader bad behavior both for the individual and other team members who learn that there are no consequences for betraying the team. That is unacceptable. We all know that.

The earlier you have these confrontational conversations, the easier they are. And the more you practice them, the better you become at them. Ultimately, it is unkind to ignore the violation of your values. It is unkind to your employee who alienates themselves from the team. It is unkind to the team because you debilitate unity and trust. It is unkind to you because you now have to pay exorbitant interest on your negligence. Clarity is kind. Clarify your values. Clarify corporate behaviors. Clarify the consequences of value violations.

8

CAST VISION

On October 12, 1971, John Lennon released the song "Imagine." It became his number one hit as a solo artist. The song details a world that approximates Revelation's final chapters: a new earth unified by love, an earth with no countries or wars, no poverty, personal possessions, or hunger. It feels like a script from Jesus' preaching. Well, it would be, except for the opening lines, which were a battle line for Lennon: "Imagine there's no heaven / It's easy if you try / No hell below us / Above us, only sky." The implication seems clear: religion is the culprit. It is the cause of wars, oppression, racism, and poverty.

But is it? There is no question that the world is full of heartache, even brutal pain. Nor is there any doubt that Christians have been complicit in the problem. The most oft-cited proof is the Crusades. Over the course of two hundred years (AD 1096–1300), there were eight distinct military campaigns to recapture the Holy Lands. Though estimates vary, an estimated two million to three million deaths are attributed to these "holy wars."

What happens if we follow Lennon's advice and excommunicate God from our geopolitics? Well, we don't have to guess. That was the experiment of socialism and communism in the twentieth century. For the twenty years surrounding World War II, estimates of the combined death toll of the regimes of China, Russia, and Germany hover around 100 million people. Do the math. Two million deaths over the two hundred years of the Crusades add up to a horrific 10,000 per year. Yet that is fractional compared to the atheistic regimes of World War II, which averaged 5 million deaths per year, or 13,699 per day! You can argue with the estimates, fudging them up or down marginally, but you cannot escape the fact that a godless world is far more brutal than the worst representation of Jesus' kingdom.

If you invert the question, the conclusion is even more striking: What positive contributions has Christianity made to humanity? Christians have been founders and forerunners in education, science, medicine, social justice, prison reform, legal systems, compassion, job creation, literacy, and women's rights.

What does all this have to do with a book on leadership and a chapter on vision? Everything! Because whether we're leading a church, a business, a nonprofit, or a home, the principles of Jesus' leadership will have transformative effects on the people we lead. When we lead with integrity, love, and sacrificial service, we make people's lives substantially better. So when we clarify the vision for the organizations we lead, we must allow Jesus' vision to shape our own by asking, "What is the ultimate destination?" I've asked Jeff to practically and pragmatically address how we ought to articulate a clear and compelling vision.

What Is Our Clear and Compelling Vision?

One would be hard-pressed to find any organization that doesn't have a vision statement. That vision statement is likely proudly displayed on plaques in conference rooms and lobbies, throughout websites, and on every employee's business card and email signature. However, if *creating* a vision statement was the heavy lifting when it comes to being a visionary leader, this leadership practice would not be the challenge it is for many leaders. But as we all know, vision is much more than a plaque on the wall or a statement you paid a handsome sum of cash to a consultant to create at a two-day, off-site session.

Vision is not a statement. It is a vivid picture that others can follow, a picture that clearly and simply defines what success looks like and inspires others to want to put in the effort *to make that vision a reality.* A well-defined vision can be used as a backdrop to help make decisions about which strategy we should consider, which investments are the most important to make, and what talent we need to hire on our team. A vivid vision allows the team to see the art of the possible, the destination we are striving for, and the driving force that motivates the extra effort necessary to be excellent. If the vision is simply an artifact that has become little more than a plaque hanging on the wall, you need to strongly reconsider what it means to create a compelling vision for your organization. A Master Leader, by definition, sits in a position of influence and operates at an altitude higher than the rest of the team. That higher altitude affords us perspective to look out into the future, see past the day-to-day tactics, and inspire the organization to achieve something great. As leaders, we take this part of our role seriously because the organization and the people we lead are counting on us to see what they don't have the ability to see.

One of the challenges with vision is that over time it tends to drift. It may be a clear and compelling vision, but like anything of great importance, it needs to be reinforced and repeated so the team doesn't lose sight of it as they work diligently to add value each day. It is easy for me to be so chin-deep into the details of a project that I forget the project's purpose. We can be so heads down that we forget to look up and get our bearings to make sure we are still on course.

When I was in the aviation industry working around pilots, they would often use metaphors about tracking toward the next waypoint. When a pilot creates a flight plan for a trip, they lay out a series of waypoints that helps them know if they're staying on course to get to the destination. Similarly, we as leaders need to help our teams by reminding them of the next waypoint that will show us if we are tracking toward our desired vision.

Master Leaders ask questions like, "Are we heading in the right direction?" "Will we have the desired impact if we achieve our vision?" and, "Are we differentiated from the others operating in our market, industry, or ministry?" Vision is not an unachievable fluffy pipe dream; it is a hunger the organization strives to pursue daily. It is the inspiration that fuels the fire in the belly of team members. Vision keeps the team moving when all odds are against them, when they are worn out and ready to quit.

At Christ's Church of the Valley, we have a simple yet compelling vision to "reach the Valley for Christ." This vision has stood the test of time. For decades, it has been an anchor. Yet it is easy—even with a simple and clear vision—to drift at times and get tangled up in the tactics of the day. We find ourselves constantly restating our vision to our congregation and staff to ensure we never lose sight of why we exist and where we're heading as a church. A few years ago, the executive team had an off-site meeting to reset our strategies and ensure we could continue to make progress toward our vision. Throughout the sessions, we bounced our strategies against our vision to make sure we didn't fall in love with a set of strategies that sounded good on paper but didn't further our vision to reach the Valley.

A clear and vivid vision will be the motivator when you're not in the room. It will speak loudly when the other voices tell the team to "do just enough to get by," to "leave it for tomorrow," or that "no one will notice anyway." Vision compels us to tap into our discretionary effort and find a way to make the vision a reality. With so many competing voices in our world and even in our own head, we need a clear voice that tells us we are set on making an impact and we will not stop until we get there. Without a compelling vision, we simply turn the crank, spin the wheel, and become mindless drones and clones doing tasks that make us feel good for a fleeting moment. We are leaders, appointed by the Most High, and he has set out an assignment for us with great meaning and purpose. Vision helps us maintain our focus on that endgame. The vision makes it all worthwhile.

Jesus' Vision: The Kingdom of God

With Jeff's advice in mind, let's examine Jesus' vision for the kingdom of God. Jesus preached and promoted the kingdom of God. His ministry began with this announcement: "The time is fulfilled, and the kingdom of God is at hand" (Mark 1:15). This was the choral refrain in all his preaching, the subject of all his parables, and the impetus of all his healings. Jesus was so clear on his vision that even a thief on the cross next to him died with this as his last request: "Jesus, remember me when you come into your kingdom" (Luke 23:42).

After the resurrection, that kingdom did come. It manifested as a group of Christ-followers, beleaguered and battered, doing the best they could to make Jesus famous. The church is the current expression of God's kingdom on earth. It is, of course, a far cry from heaven. But that is merely the earthly reality in the present realm. God's kingdom, as described in Revelation 21–22, is far grander, even greater than Lennon's "Imagine" ditty.

Many have drawn a hard line between the church, God's kingdom on earth, and the kingdom to come in the new heaven and new earth. It is as if the purpose of the church is to get people to heaven. Let me be clear: that is *not* the purpose of the church. The purpose of the church is to bring heaven to earth. This comes straight from Jesus' lips in the Lord's Prayer: "Your kingdom come, your will be done *on earth* as it is in heaven" (Matt. 6:10).

The purpose of the church is to bring heaven to earth.

Can we fully bring God's kingdom to fruition on this earth? No. Obviously not. But perhaps we could make others' hell on earth a bit more like heaven and inspire them to change eternal zip codes in the process. How do we do that? By being crystal clear about God's original intentions—his original vision for his creation. To understand the kingdom of God, we need to return to the creation of the world.

Jesus didn't just want to take us forward to a desired destination *someday*. He wanted to take us backward to God's original intention *today*. There is a fancy word for that—recapitulation. It basically means that we go forward by circling back. As Westerners, we think of history as linear. We even talk about "timelines." We see progress as moving forward. Traditional Jewish thinking saw history as cyclical: what happened before will circle back again (think *The Lion King* and the "Circle of Life"). Progress doesn't develop in a straight line but in a spiral that can move upward or downward.

In Jesus' day, Jewish historians believed they were in a downward spiral due to Roman occupation. They had, of course, seen that cycle before in Babylon, Assyria, and Egypt. Jesus wanted to reverse the spiral to move us upward to God's original plan. We see this clearly in Revelation 22, which describes our future as a return to the Eden of Genesis 2: "Then the angel showed me the river of the water of life, bright as crystal, flowing from the throne of God and of the Lamb through the middle of the street of the city; also, on either side of the river, the tree of life with its twelve kinds of fruit, yielding its fruit each month. The leaves of the tree were for the healing of the nations" (Rev. 22:1–2).

In Jesus' day, the liberation from Roman oppression would require circling back to the Exodus itself, where Israel took a detour. Jesus would lead them on the true path. For example, Israel wandered for forty years in the wilderness because of their lack of faith. Jesus, in contrast, would undergo temptation in the wilderness for a mere forty days without succumbing to Satan's temptations. The temple in Jerusalem was supposed to be the place where God met his people. However, in Jesus' day, it had been defiled by Roman occupation and Sadducean concession. Jesus, knowing it needed an overhaul, predicted going back to the foundation: "Destroy this temple, and in three days I will raise it up" (John 2:19).

As extraordinary as that claim was, it was the tip of the iceberg. Jesus claimed to be the embodied fulfillment of virtually everything important to Israel. He was the recapitulation of God's presence in the temple, God's Word in the Torah, and God's redemption in the Passover lamb. We see this most powerfully in how Jesus embodied the Sabbath itself—established in Eden by God himself: "And on the seventh day God finished the work that he had done, and he rested on the seventh day from all his work that he had done. So God blessed the seventh day and made it holy, because on it God rested from all his work that he had done in creation" (Gen. 2:2–3). Jesus had the audacity to claim he was the Lord of the Sabbath (Mark 2:28). It would be difficult to overemphasize the weight of these claims.

Jesus came to establish God's kingdom on earth. He knew it would ultimately be fraught with imperfections and failures along the way. But he was trying to bring a bit of heaven to earth by circling back to God's intention in Eden. Consider his words: "Truly I tell you, at *the renewal of all things*, when the Son of Man sits on his glorious throne, you who have followed me will also sit on twelve thrones, judging the twelve tribes of Israel" (Matt. 19:28, NIV).

His agenda was clear: return humanity to its rightful place under God. His death on the cross removed the barrier of the Law so that God's children could sit at his feet once again, enjoying the fellowship of the Father in the beauty of a garden. That begins now! And you can be a participant in God's kingdom through your leadership. Ultimately, we will not achieve Jesus' full vision until we reach the new heaven and new earth. Nonetheless, here and now we are his envoys, casting his vision of a preferred future wherein God and man are at peace again. Our destiny is not a doctrine, not a set of beliefs, but an experience with God, a way of being human.

We can participate in God's kingdom through our leadership.

How can we leverage our leadership to bring a bit of heaven to earth? By loving people when they are unlovely. Providing jobs and dignity. Helping our followers find purpose. Holding people to higher standards and forgiving them when they fail. Confessing our own failures. Modeling resilience. This list could extend to thousands of specific bullet points. Bottom line, we imitate the Master in bringing a bit of heaven to people's hell on earth. There is still a bit of Eden to be had here before we go to the New Jerusalem there.

Chapter Summary

Vision is to an organization what a bull's-eye is to an archer. If your team knows what you're aiming at, you will empower them to make progress toward it. That's why it's so critical we be clear and concise, memorable and motivational. For Christian leaders, however, there is another layer. Jesus calls us to be salt and light—to bring heaven to earth today—so that we can bring souls from earth to heaven someday. Allowing Jesus' vision to mark your vision statement will add depth, purpose, and power to your organization. Of course, no matter how great your vision is, it won't matter without an effective strategy to carry it out. That's where we're headed in the next chapter.

TAKE ACTION ON CASTING VISION

A Master Leader's primary task is articulating a clear and compelling vision of a preferred future. So where do we start? Our vision must align with the Master's. However, each of us plays a unique local role in expanding the kingdom, leading to the renewal of Eden. Here are several exercises I hope you'll use to help you clarify your vision, both individually and for the church or organization you lead.

Vision Statement

Craft an Inspirational and Sticky Vision Statement

Your vision statement must meet four criteria. It must be succinct, clear, memorable, and motivational. Let's look at each one:

Succinct. An effective vision statement must be portable. If it doesn't fit on a bumper sticker, it won't stick.

Clear. It must precisely describe the preferred future you want to lead people toward.

Memorable. The turn of phrase must turn heads. If it doesn't, it isn't likely that people use it as a choral refrain with members and constituents.

Motivational. Your vision statement should move people to action. It must pack a power punch of emotion. By tapping into people's hearts, we can engage their hands and feet.

Let's get started. Mark off one hour in your calendar during the time of day you have the highest level of energy. Get a drink, turn off your phone, open your journal, and prepare to write. But for the first thirty minutes, *do not write anything.* Just sit and visualize: If the kingdom of God were to incarnate in your organization successfully, how would your community look different five years from now? What would the families you serve have that they don't have now? What would those outside your organization say about your organization behind your back? What problems do people face today that they would not have to face five years from now if you fulfilled your mission?

Over the next fifteen minutes, write only single words or phrases. Then take another fifteen minutes to summarize your phrases in a single paragraph describing the preferred future five years from now if your organization is successful with its mission. Then leave it.

In a week, revisit what you've written. Distill the vivid description of your future into a concise statement, highlighting key phrases and sentences. Now reduce the highlighted ideas into a single sentence. Share what you've developed with two or three confidants and wrestle with it word by word. Rewrite it and make it so sticky it won't be easy to forget. (Note: this rewrite might take weeks or even months.) Share it with confidants. Test it with critics and stakeholders. Revisit it weekly. The end product should be simple, straightforward enough to understand, and compelling enough to inspire action. It's worth the time to get this right. It is the road sign that points to your future destination.

Vision Alignment

Evaluate Your Organizational Assets and Liabilities Through the Lens of Your Vision

Exercise #1: Gather the key stakeholders you've confided in throughout the process of crafting your vision statement. Share with them the finished product. It should be familiar to all of them since they were a part of creating and critiquing it along the way. Ask them about their current actions and behaviors that promote the vision.

Caution #1: don't ask what they're doing that *does not* align with the vision. It's too soon and too threatening to get an honest answer. Caution #2: don't interrupt or respond; let them speak! You need all your mental energy to focus and listen to their response. How they answer this question will tell you where the most significant assets and greatest potential liabilities are in your organization. Thank them for their input. Take some time to sit with it and let it simmer. Think through people's answers, their vocal inflections, where they got excited, and when they got defensive. Your sole goal in this exercise is to expose both opportunities and liabilities for the vision (not for you—for the vision).

Exercise #2: List your greatest vision assets under three headings: People (employees and volunteers), Programs (things you practice and produce), and Resources (financial, physical, and social—culture, momentum, advocates, etcetera). Next, list your greatest vision liabilities under the same categories. The gap between these two lists is the change needed in the organization. Take these lists to your two to three key advisors (board members, executives, or supporters). Ask for their opinion about what might be missing or incorrectly categorized.

Exercise #3: Prioritize both lists. Rank your assets and liabilities from greatest to least. Once ordered, put an asterisk by items that are urgent to change. The most important may not be the most urgent. There might be a minor issue you can or should address immediately to stop some bleeding so that the more important things can be done with less cost or damage. Take your priorities and urgencies to your two to three advisors for their assessment. Once you account for their feedback, you now have an action plan for moving the organization forward in a specific direction.

I've drawn a lot of insight about systems and vision from author and pastor Andy Stanley. He says that every system unconsciously conspires to maintain the status quo and prevent change.[13] Systems, by their very nature, maintain equilibrium. That, of course, is a good thing. Our entire physical and mental makeup craves consistency to counterbalance the chaos of life. However, when a system stands in the way of necessary progress, it conspires against us. Psychologists have proven that people spend more energy avoiding pain than seeking pleasure. That observation explains, in part, why the people you lead would rather you keep an ineffective system. For example, everyone groans when the organization announces a new operating system. "Ugh!" rings out across the staff meeting even though they complain about the present system. Why? Because change disrupts equilibrium.

Nonetheless, the core of leadership is moving people from where they are to a desired future. Movement of any kind is change. It will be resisted instinctively as a survival mechanism. A Master Leader fights for change. However, you must figure out how to make the move with the least discomfort and disruption. Though there are many available strategies for that, explaining the "why" is undoubtedly your greatest ally. If you're unwilling or unable to lead in change, you cannot lead at the highest level. It's that simple. If you're cringing reading this, perhaps you would benefit from author John Kotter's 1996 business classic, *Leading Change.*

Change costs the leader. It costs you influence and loyalty every time you make a change. It may not be wise to clean the slate in one afternoon. You must have enough leadership credits in your organizational account to cover the cost of each change. *If your leadership account goes negative, the organization will change you rather than you changing the organization.* Read that sentence again. Many leaders are removed because they do the right thing the wrong way. They force positive change, which causes them to go negative in their leadership clout account. You have signed your exit papers when you do that.

One last observation from Craig Groeschel: people don't dislike change; they dislike the way you try to change them. We all embrace change: clothes, furniture, new technology, etcetera. When change becomes difficult, it feels imposing (forced upon me), confusing (I don't know what the fallout will be), or irrational (I don't understand why the change is made). By using clear communication and ensuring alignment to the mission, we can minimize the disruption of necessary and ultimately welcomed change.

9

DEVELOP STRATEGY

At the beginning of the 2015–2016 Premier League soccer season, Leicester City had 5,000:1 odds of winning the championship. If you're prone to indulge in DraftKings or FanDuel, this is *not* a bet you would want to make. Nobody in their right mind would have given the team manager, Claudio Ranieri, any chance to take home the cup at the end of the season. However, he recognized that he had two players with extraordinary speed, Jamie Vardy and Riyad Mahrez. He came up with an unprecedented strategy to leverage this advantage, as minimal as it was in the overall game.

He coached the team to drop their defense deep into the backfield but then quickly release a counterattack when they regained possession. It required risk. They had to allow their opponents to swarm their goal and gain a numerical advantage. But once Leicester City regained possession, they quickly sent the ball long into their opponent's field, where their defenders were stretched thin due to the attack. This allowed their two fastest strikers more one-on-one opportunities to score. This surprising strategy was so successful that Leicester City won the Premier League in 2016 in one of the most astonishing underdog stories in sports history.

The right strategy at the right time can have an outsized impact on your success. Jeff knows a thing or two about developing strategy. So before I walk through the biblical strategy of shepherds, I've asked him to talk about how top-tier leaders develop strategy.

How Do Top Leaders Develop Strategy?

Master Leaders have a clear vision and know the destination they want to lead the team or organization toward. Once we have established a clear and compelling vision, as well as the destination, let's determine how we will actually get to that destination. In other words, what path will you take to get to the desired destination?

Often, we as leaders overcomplicate vision, mission, strategy, and objectives. Here's the way I like to explain how all these concepts work together in a simple, aligned fashion: Our *vision* is our desired destination; it's where we want to be in the future. The *mission* is simply why we exist as an organization—our main purpose. The *strategies* are the paths we will take to get to that destination. Finally, the *objectives* or annual goals are the milestones we want to complete in a certain time frame to ensure we're staying on course to reach our destination. That may sound simple, but I have to keep reminding myself of the differences of each element so that I can have a clear picture of how to lead and guide the team along the journey.

Strategies can sometimes be seen as pie-in-the-sky ideals of what we might accomplish in some perfect scenario or future state. Master Leaders realize the importance of having clear strategies to help guide the team and make sure they don't find themselves chasing a series of initiatives that don't align or track toward the vision. When done well, strategies do much more than help us stay focused on the right path; they also help us say no to the many opportunities that could be distractions from keeping the main thing the main thing.

I remember when I was a new general manager for a product line, and I had my first exposure to a comprehensive annual strategy plan. I had been running the product line for about nine months, and we were very profitable and maintained strong client satisfaction with our products. My days were consumed primarily with engineering-design setbacks, manufacturing issues, and supply chain challenges.

I walked into the conference room where the strategic planning session was scheduled to take place over the next four hours. Sitting in front of us were three-inch binders filled with graphs and slides that talked about emerging technology trends, S.W.O.T. (Strength, Weakness, Opportunity, Threat) analysis, client-stakeholder scenarios, and at least ten different financial outlooks for the next five years. I can't even guess how many hours of work and effort went into crafting this strategy document, but I can tell you how often that large binder was opened in the year that followed. You guessed it: zero! That strategy document sat pristinely on the shelf of my office as I went back to working on the operational issues that caused my clients concern and frustration. This cycle continued each and every year and created in my eyes a very negative view of the value of strategy.

So many times, the example I just outlined is how most people view strategies. It is unfortunate because I have learned since then that strategy development is one of the most powerful tools in a leader's toolbelt. Sitting down with our teams and talking through the possible paths we can take to make forward progress toward achieving our vision is actually quite energizing. Once we lay out the potential paths or strategies we might take and talk through each one, we can typically agree very quickly on which path is best to take and begin refining the strategy until we feel it can be executed. If done well, strategies will last many years and won't likely change much unless there is a significant event or disruption that changes the industry or ministry we are serving. Strategy development is an essential part of our leadership role. The key is to keep it simple and only change it when absolutely necessary.

Being a strategic leader is an important step in giving our teams the confidence that they can be successful and the knowledge that they are on track to make progress toward the vision. Any leader can be strategic if we just take the time to chart the course we feel is best, get input from our team and other leaders, and ensure we have the resources to execute the selected strategy. While leaders who are more tactical in nature may struggle a bit in this area, the key to being strategic is not intellect but simple intentionality. Just allow yourself space to plan and time to think about the vision and the path to get there.

Remember, great leaders know they don't have all the answers. They consult the wisdom of Scripture and seek wise counsel. Becoming a strategic leader is simple. It may not always be easy, but it is simple. *Find the path that will best get you and your team to the desired destination.* Mark will now take these principles back to the Bible.

The Strategy of the Shepherd

In the Bible, the primary leadership model was a shepherd. When the apostle Paul coached the leaders of the church of Ephesus (Acts 20:17–35), he used that metaphor to give them specific strategies for leadership. There are four primary obligations of a shepherd in ancient Israel: leading, feeding, healing, and protecting. Let's look at four key insights from Scripture to suggest specific leadership strategies for our modern settings:

1. *Lead the flock.* Shepherds are always thinking forward to where the flock needs to go next. They already see the still waters and green pastures where their flock can grow and thrive. Likewise, strategic planning is an essential skill for Master Leaders. Not only do we need to clearly see a preferred future, but we also need to know the steps it will take to get the flock there. It begins by setting achievable goals that lead to the fulfillment of the mission. The vision will inspire people to action, but its magnitude may also paralyze participants along the way. As leaders, we bridge the gap with realistic and incremental goals. Our goals should stretch people to do more than they thought they could but also be manageable with the time and

resources at their disposal. As leaders, it's our responsibility to map out the mission with concrete goals that drive directly to the mission. This takes time and deliberate attention.

Many leaders are too frenetic in managing their day to meditate on the future. Perhaps you can relate. However, if you can't create space for visioneering, you will sentence yourself to management as a substitute for leadership. As a rule, quality strategic planning will take an entire day every year, a half-day each month, and a couple of hours every week. Simply put, it requires mental margin to map achievable goals (see the Goal Creation exercise at the end of this chapter).

Sometimes the most strategic move is not to add programs or products but to remove barriers to those you already offer. Most churches (and businesses) think about adding programs or products to attract people. Attractional programs and products reach far fewer with more effort and resources than simply *removing barriers*. Ask, "What could hinder people from coming?" before asking, "What else could draw them in?" For example, if you want to reach teens, you might want to reword your messaging, update your social media presence, or change your service times. If you want to attract a specific ethnic group, then skin color on stage, verbal expressions, and physical touch might be important. If you want to attract senior citizens, then the pace of speaking, the volume of music, and the physical accessibility of seats is critical.

Adding programs and products reaches fewer people than simply removing barriers.

2. *Feed the flock.* Shepherds don't feed their sheep. They strategically guide them to a safe environment where the sheep can naturally nourish themselves. The parallel for a pastor is not to spoon feed the flock. Instead, our strategy is to give them the tools to feed themselves. In other words, we should be more like coaches than professors. Our sermons should be oriented to personal application rather than academic information. It's not so different for leaders of

other organizations. Leaders are at their best when they empower people to grow themselves.

Therefore, we should invest in programs that add value. In the church, value-add programs are easy to identify: Are people eager to invite a work colleague or a pre-Christian friend to a worship service or outreach event? Do you have to explain the importance of the event or merely inform people how to register to ensure they reserve a spot? The answers indicate whether your programs are adding value. Check out these examples: A daddy/daughter dance is a huge win for fathers. A sexual purity event for preteens takes a lot of pressure off parents. Sports leagues, marriage retreats, financial planning, and grief support—they all offer value to people wrestling with real-life issues.

3. *Heal the flock.* In Psalm 23:4, the psalmist sings, "Your rod and your staff, they comfort me." These were the shepherd's tools of the trade. The *staff* was used to guide and prod the sheep in the right direction. The *rod* was a weapon to fight predators. It was also a tool to part the sheep's wool to check for hidden abrasions and parasites. A shepherd must be vigilant to care for their flock. That's why Paul coached his leaders to "pay careful attention to yourselves and to all the flock, in which the Holy Spirit has made you overseers, to care for the church of God, which he obtained with his own blood" (Acts 20:28).

If you lead people in any capacity, you know they come with a labyrinth of family dysfunction, sexual baggage, addictions, childhood trauma, relational triage, sickness, death, and financial crisis. Most of these issues don't surface in daily interactions. They surface through complaints, apathy, absenteeism, or conflict. Leaders develop strategies for identifying and solving the problem beneath the problem. The flock can only be healthy if you strategically "part the wool." That requires proximity; as Brad Lomenick says, "You can impress people from a distance, but you can only influence them up close."[14]

One way to part the wool is to create a feedback culture. Many organizations are unhealthy because they have never been diagnosed. To get better, we must provide timely and actionable feedback to our teams. It must be *timely* because it will be too late to learn from the feedback by the time the annual review rolls around. And it must be *actionable* because, without knowing how to course-correct, your feedback is simply criticism. Behavioral feedback feels more like coaching than criticism, and coaching is far easier to receive than criticism (see the Feedback Protocol exercise at the end of this chapter).

There is neither rod nor staff without hard conversations. No one likes to have difficult conversations. But the reality is that no one gets better without them. Sociologists have found that they are even more difficult for those working in churches and nonprofits, where it is common to confuse being kind with being nice.[15] Clarity is kindness. In light of that, here is a strategic template you can adopt and adapt:

a. Begin by affirming the individual's inherent worth and value to the team.
b. State that this conversation will be difficult, but you are willing to have it because you value *them*, their *reputation* in the organization, and their *effectiveness* on the team.
c. Identify the behavior *and* the consequences flowing from it. For example, "You keep showing up late for meetings. This makes others feel devalued because you disrespect their time."
d. Provide measurable steps to help them change the behavior(s), as well as a plan for scheduled follow-up meetings to monitor their progress. You might even allow them to contribute to or construct these steps: "I have some suggestions for improvement, but I would first like to hear ideas you have for making helpful changes." This kind of approach helps them understand the problem and gives them buy-in on the solution.

e. Conclude by reaffirming their value to you and the organization and asking for their feedback to see where there might be misalignment or misunderstanding.

These don't have to be long meetings, but they do have to be clear. Five minutes is often sufficient. Some people need time to evaluate and adjust to your critique—they may not be capable of receiving it immediately. Don't judge their receptiveness by their initial response. Give it a couple of days to a week to let them think about it and a second opportunity to share their feedback.

4. *Protect the flock.* Every shepherd knows there are wolves. But according to Paul, they are not the enemy "out there." He clearly said the wolves would rise up from "among your own selves" (Acts 20:29–31). The greatest barrier to any organization lies within its own ranks. Many people would love to experience the connection of your church or the value of your organization. Yet when they come, they are treated as an outsider, not embraced as an insider. To shift your organization, you, as the leader, need to make two strategic shifts.

First, shift your mindset from individuals to groups. Most leaders cater to key constituents. This could be the largest contributors, the loudest critics, or their closest friends. Leaders do not have the luxury of catering to individuals. We must ask relentlessly, "What is best for the organization?" Don Wilson, the founding pastor of Christ's Church of the Valley, modeled this as well as any leader I've ever met. During one building campaign, a man offered Don a check for a million dollars if he would put the man's name on the building. Without hesitation, Pastor Don refused, simply saying, "We don't do that." No organization can excel if individuals are the primary concern over the organization.

Second, deal with the little problems before they become big ones. Most big problems were once small enough to ignore. If you are unwilling to deal with the consequences of the big problem later, do the diligent and difficult task of attacking it early.[16] The key to solving problems before they loom large is identifying the "why" behind the "what." Why is she late to every meeting? Why did the team not adequately prepare for the event? Why were the elderly complaining about the music? This secret motivates Master Leaders to solve little problems before they become big ones: every problem has an opportunity hidden in it when you have a strategy to manage it. Don't procrastinate the gain you could achieve by solving this problem.

> **Problems are hidden opportunities when you have strategies to manage them.**

Chapter Summary

Without a clear vision, you don't know where you're leading people. And without an actionable strategy, you won't have a road map to take them there. Your strategy will be specific to your organization and setting. Nonetheless, we can draw from the shepherd metaphor in the Bible some clear categories of strategies surrounding leading, feeding, healing, and protecting your flock. By thinking and acting both biblically and strategically, we can become the Master Leaders God has called us to be. That is, of course, if we focus on the right priorities, which is the conversation for the next chapter.

TAKE ACTION ON DEVELOPING STRATEGY

Building an effective strategy requires us to establish goals and create a culture that values feedback. Goals that are realistic but difficult will stretch the team to accomplish more with less. Feedback helps the team improve both the goals and the implementation of those goals. The following two action steps will help guide your implementation of these key strategy components.

Goal Creation

Identify and Prioritize Goals, Objectives, and Assessments

Gather your key leaders for an all-day planning session. Print your organization's vision and mission statements and post them on a wall so that every goal is directed toward these statements.

Step #1: Brainstorm three five-year goals. Then break them down into one-year goals and further into quarterly goals. Each goal must be achievable, measurable, and on target for your mission.

Step #2: Add clarifiers for each goal. 1) A *champion* who will take ownership of accomplishing that goal. 2) A list of *advocates* who will build a team to accomplish each goal. 3) The *resources* necessary to achieve the goal—human, material, financial, technological, etcetera. 4) *Challenges* that could impede progress toward the goal. 5) A *target date* for completion of the goal.

Step #3: Break down each goal into incremental objectives. Make them SMART (Specific, Measurable, Achievable, Relevant, Time-bound). These specific objectives become the mile-markers along the way to the successful achievement of the goals. They will tell you whether you need more gas, more resources, or more people.

Step #4: Develop Key Performance Indicators (KPIs). This will help you know whether and to what extent the goal has been achieved. Set a target of three to five KPIs for each goal. These can be quantitative (e.g., revenue growth, customer acquisition, teacher/student ratios) or qualitative (e.g., customer satisfaction, team morale, clarity of vision). What gets measured gets repeated. After the all-day session, follow up on what you did together. Over the coming weeks, you'll want to prioritize steps 5 and 6.

Step #5: Schedule regular check-ins. The more precise your KPIs, the shorter your meetings. These check-ins aim to catch your team doing something right and celebrate the wins. This also allows you to adjust strategies or KPIs as needed.

Step #6: Document and communicate. Clear communication keeps everyone on the same page and moving in the same direction.

Every stakeholder should know precisely where the team stands. Remember, strategy is never set in stone. You can adjust goals up or down based on altered circumstances, accelerated achievements, changes in personnel, or unforeseen challenges. Frequent iterations are normal so long as your KPIs are clear, your communication is regular, and the mission is front and center.

Feedback Protocol

Construct a Culture of Constructive Critique

If the key leader doesn't seek feedback, no one below them will feel free to create a feedback culture. And it's not just your responsibility to seek feedback; it is also your responsibility to train people in *how* to seek feedback. Furthermore, if feedback is not a scheduled rhythm, it will feel personal rather than professionally helpful. Here are some actionable steps for effectively seeking feedback.

Step #1: Ask for specifics. Ask people to look for very specific things prior to a performance. If it is a message or a speech, you could ask them to look for places you need to speed up or slow down. Ask another person to identify any potential cultural misunderstandings that could lead to offense. Ask another to assess your facial expressions or hand gestures. People will offer far more helpful critiques if they know what to look for.

Step #2: Never defend; always thank. As soon as you defend yourself, you are critiquing the critique. You should *always* critique the critique, but never publicly and not while it's being given. Consider critique as one person's perspective of how you could get better. Whether you make any changes is up to you. However, if you *never* course-correct based on critique, you will communicate to everyone that their opinion has no value. By only responding to the critiques you consider helpful, you'll train others to offer better, more focused critiques in the future. And by thanking them, you are making it safe to give deeper critique going forward.

Step #3: Schedule regular feedback moments. This could be right after a talk. It could be an after-action review. It could be during monthly one-on-one meetings. But if it's not a regular rhythm, it will feel more like a personal attack than a helpful critique.

Step #4: Celebrate the action taken on feedback. When the feedback is helpful and you alter your next performance because of it, recognize the person who gave you the feedback to improve you. Focus the attention on the team getting better, not you personally looking better. They should know that you care more about the organization's success than your own reputation. Critique then becomes not merely safe but also a path to career advancement. When someone builds up the organization, they will be elevated in it. Feedback is intimidating, so for it to become natural and embedded into your culture, you'll need to consistently reinforce it.

10

FOCUS PRIORITIES

On June 6, 1944, the United States unleashed an unprecedented force of 6,939 naval vessels, over 10,440 aircraft, 450,000 tons of ammunition, and 156,115 troops. That was day one. Today, this strategic attack, originally known as Operation Overlord, is simply called D-Day. This massive concentration of troops and resources was, according to many historians, the turning point of World War II.

Operation Overlord was a high-stakes gamble for President Eisenhower because it funneled such a vast amount of the Allies' military resources into a single, concentrated effort. Failure could have been catastrophic, prolonging the war or even ensuring victory for the Nazis. What President Eisenhower knew, however, was that success on D-Day would force Hitler to fight on two fronts, dividing his resources and ensuring his defeat. And the rest, as they say, is history.

This illustrates the power of focus. Too many leaders attempt too many things. By focusing our energy and resources on our greatest strength, we accomplish more by doing less. Good leaders are often visionaries, seeing further into the future and more broadly in the present. That's their strength. But *great* leaders, Master Leaders, learn to harness their vision into a pointed focus. A laser beam of leadership will go farther than a shotgun of activity.

At the time of this writing, Christ's Church of the Valley has sixteen campuses across the Phoenix Valley and a staff of more than five hundred. We could do all kinds of good things. We don't. We don't do homeless ministry, women's ministry, racial reconciliation rallies, AA, after-school programs, etcetera. Oh, don't misunderstand. Our people do all those things. But as a staff, we have focused our energy and resources on only four things: weekend service, kids and student programming, groups, and sports ministry. That's it. Why? Because we realize that by doing less, we can do more, releasing our people to accomplish the multitude of ministries God has equipped them to pursue.

The secret to doing more is not the breadth of your efforts but rather the depth. Jesus modeled that with his own narrow focus. He never preached against slavery or for women's rights, though both were desperate needs of his day. He didn't do prison ministry, campaign for the right to life, or offer marriage retreats. Yet you know as well as I do that his ministry dramatically impacted all those critical issues. Jesus' depth of focus on the kingdom of God resulted in a breadth of impact in the world. Before we unpack that in the biblical text, Jeff is going to coach us on the power of focus for leaders in contemporary settings.

The Power of Focus

You may be familiar with the idea of focusing on the vital few versus the trivial many. Focus is often used to help us to stay on point, to keep our eye on the prize. Why is this leadership action of focusing our priorities so difficult? After all, it just makes sense. I propose this may be one of the most difficult leadership principles to master, not because we don't understand the importance of focus but because we simply lack the discipline to remain focused, as distractions come at us from every angle. In the previous chapter, we talked about the importance of developing effective strategies to help us say no to opportunities that may be good but not the best option. It is a critical leadership principle that as we narrow our focus, we broaden our impact.

While you, like me, might love simplicity, my guess is it probably eludes your grip most of the time. Think about it: we admire organizations with a clear and focused vision, as well as leaders who know what they want to accomplish. They target goals with precision and have a clear plan of action. Think about the successful hamburger chain In-N-Out Burger. Their menu is simple—burgers, fries, and shakes. That's it. They have resisted the temptation to try to be all things to all people; they just do burgers and fries really well. They keep their menu simple and their focus strong.

Even from a young age, we admire people who know what they want to do when they grow up—like becoming a firefighter, a doctor, a musician, a teacher, or a pastor. But many of us have no idea what we want to accomplish with that level of specificity. Perhaps we want to leave all our options open or just not be too quick to commit to a defined course of action. But when we do this, we forgo the work needed to identify a clear destination or game plan that will help us know what to say yes and no to. That's fine when you're four or fourteen or even in your early twenties, but as your career grows, your focus should narrow. The same is true for your company or organization. Without focus, your team can be paralyzed.

I say all this knowing that people are wired differently. For some, focus is natural. For others, it can be a real struggle. Your risk tolerance and entrepreneurial spirit can greatly affect your ability to maintain a clear and present focus. If you have a high risk tolerance and entrepreneurial mindset, focus will be a huge challenge for you. You'll be more inclined to surround yourself with every possible option and do your best to pursue each one. For many organizations, this level of opportunity is a huge strength as it relates to creativity, innovation, and continuous improvement.

Now if your leadership style is more risk-averse with a greater fear of failure, you have the opposite problem. You tend to take all safe bets that don't really move the needle. If this is your leadership leaning, you'll need to work on expanding your focus a bit and taking a few more swings so that you don't become crippled by fear of failure or become a leader without inspiration that no one will be compelled to follow.

When I was in my mid-thirties, I remember being proud of my ability to multitask. I felt like this was a skill set I could really leverage as I grew my career and expanded my scope of responsibility. I loved the challenge of seeing how many plates I could keep spinning and relished the fact that I almost never had to say no to any project or challenge. Mastering the art of multitasking allowed me to deliver on commitment after commitment and show my leaders I was ready to keep moving up in my responsibility. I thought for sure I had found the recipe for how to be a high producer in a dog-eats-dog corporate culture.

Then it happened. The headhunter called me and recruited me into a role with responsibility for clients and tens of thousands of employees all across the globe. It took me less than three months to realize this model I had learned and was so confident in was unable to scale at the next level and was unsustainable in terms of delivering great results and maintaining a healthy work-life balance. It was time to get serious about focus.

I had built a career around operational excellence and the discipline of efficiencies and cost improvements. I could apply these skills really well to products and services, but I wasn't leveraging those same disciplines of focus in my career and life. I began using the tenets of Lean Six Sigma (it would be worth your time to look it up). I prioritized no more than three key inputs for each output I wanted to achieve. I reduced everything to the factor of three: the top three clients I wanted to ensure I spent the majority of my time on; the top three members of my team who needed my time and energy; the top three areas of leadership I wanted to improve on, etcetera. As I began to limit my focus to the vital few, I began to increase my impact overall. I delegated more, trusted my team more, and surprisingly found I was able to have more balance and more success than I thought possible. I went from being a shotgun to a rifle to a laser. It made all the difference.

The challenge for us as Master Leaders will be limiting the options we pursue and where we place our precious investment of the time, talent, and resources we use going after potential opportunities. There is a group of leaders out there with an appetite to be all things to all people that drives them to be unfocused and unclear. As Stephen Covey says, "The key is not to prioritize what's on your schedule, but to schedule your priorities."[17] With the number of distractions that naturally bombard us as leaders today, making focus one of our primary areas to invest in as a leader is masterful. Mark will now walk through what that focus looked like for Jesus. Perhaps his model will help you shape your own leadership focus on what mattered most to the Master.

Jesus' Focus of Power: God's Kingdom

Jesus' vision—his desired destination—was crystal clear: the kingdom of God. As I mentioned in chapter 8, he was narrowly focused on the nature of that vision. In this chapter, however, I will address his *focus* on that vision. It started at the very beginning of his ministry (Mark 1:15) and permeated his preaching until his brutal assassination (Matt. 4:23; 9:35; Luke 4:43; 8:1; 9:11). The phrase "kingdom of God" appears 106 times in the Gospels. That's a lot! It's the epicenter of Jesus' vision. This *is* the point of his preaching and the purpose of his parables . . . all of them!

Because Jesus talked so frequently about the kingdom of God, it must have been a common conversation in his day. Right? Actually, no, not even close. Only rarely is the kingdom mentioned by other teachers and writers of the time. Jesus *alone* prioritized the kingdom. Only on rare occasions did other rabbis speak about the kingdom, and when they did, it was merely wishful thinking about a potential, future dream. Jesus alone asserted the kingdom as a present reality. In fact, that was the whole point of Jesus' preaching: "The time is fulfilled, and the kingdom of God is at hand; repent and believe in the gospel" (Mark 1:15).

As leaders who follow our Master, we must allow his focus to permeate our priorities. The kingdom of God may sound spiritual or ethereal, but it is all too real. It is here and now, and it is day to day. Some see the kingdom of God as a mere future reality (that was the mistake of Jesus' contemporaries as well). It is seen as some fuzzy idea of getting to heaven someday or something hidden in our hearts, like a personal faith. Talk of the kingdom of God is confined to sermons on Sunday when the preacher cracks open the Bible. But the kingdom is far broader than an hour on Sunday morning.

We must allow our Master's focus to permeate our priorities.

God's kingdom—Jesus' focus—expands when our businesses provide goods and services to improve families; when we create jobs and healthcare for our workers; when we orchestrate a safe and inclusive work environment; or when we improve education, medical care, care for the environment, or mental health support. All of that has kingdom impact by bringing a bit of heaven to earth. Where did we come up with that idea? It actually stems from the leadership model Jesus showed us. Let's look at three key observations.

1. *Jesus envisioned a community of God's covenant people.* Jesus would stand at the head of this one nation under God. Why does that matter to us today? Because we are not merely trying to get people to heaven. As I mentioned in chapter 8, we are attempting to bring a bit of heaven to earth. We have a vision in the real world, one we need to focus on. Thus, it's not only religious leaders who are needed to expand and extend God's kingdom. Jesus built a church in which everyone was a priest of God. As the apostle Peter observed, "You yourselves like living stones are being built up as a spiritual

house, to be a *holy priesthood*, to offer spiritual sacrifices acceptable to God through Jesus Christ" (1 Pet. 2:5).

This idea of the priesthood of all believers goes back to a command God gave right *before* giving the Ten Commandments: "You shall be to me a kingdom of priests and a holy nation" (Exod. 19:6). It was *always* God's intent that all his people would be priests. All who called on his name would be called into his service to build his kingdom on this earth. Unfortunately, Israel failed in her vocation. She replaced the sovereign God with an earthly king and reduced the priesthood to a designated clan of specialists. These actions thwarted the influence of the nation and truncated the kingdom of God. We dare not make the same mistake as we race toward the finish line of the Great Commission. All who call on the name of Jesus must imitate the Master and lead with his priority of building God's kingdom on earth until he comes.

We need Master Leaders in finance and education, athletics and politics, and construction and technology. Without community and industry leaders aligning with Jesus' kingdom, our impact will be minimized. Those at the top of their industry, under the leadership of Jesus, will have the broadest impact in the community. With this in mind, let's usher in a second observation critical to Jesus' vision of the kingdom.

The leaders who align with Jesus' kingdom will have the broadest impact.

2. *The kingdom of Israel had been a failure.* The original political plan for Israel was a theocracy. Yahweh alone would be king: "For the LORD is our judge; the LORD is our lawgiver; the LORD is our king; he will save us" (Isa. 33:22). This idea was so strong that the establishment of the monarchy was equated to the rejection of Yahweh (1 Sam. 8:7).

What Israel really wanted in a king was military protection. They trusted a human warrior more than an invisible God. The monarchy stood in constant tension in Israel because it naturally subverted the sole rule of Yahweh. Bottom line: God was the rightful ruler of Israel, but Israel demanded a more tangible king. Are we not doing the same thing when we trust in our industry more than our Creator? As a leader, in whatever field, we represent God's agenda. We dare not make the same mistake as ancient Israel and put our trust in worldly institutions rather than King Jesus, who reigns over every nation and in every industry. It may require courage to bring God's rule into our industry or field, but if that was the narrow focus of Jesus while he walked the earth, should it not be the driving priority for those of us who follow the Master Leader?

3. *God's king had to seek God's heart.* God instructs Samuel to anoint David as king: "Do not look on his appearance or on the height of his stature, because I have rejected him. For the LORD sees not as man sees: man looks on the outward appearance, but the LORD looks on the heart" (1 Sam. 16:7).

David became the quintessential leader of Israel precisely because he left leadership in the hands of Yahweh, Israel's ultimate king. He was merely God's servant to point God's people to God's laws. His goal was God's fame, not his own. He battled for God's honor, not his own reputation. *That* is the kind of leader God is looking for.

However, as we know, David was also flawed on multiple levels, as we all are. His flaws did not disqualify him from being a leader, but ultimately, he was incapable of ruling God's dynasty permanently. For this, we needed Jesus Christ. David thus became the imperfect model after which the messianic hopes were fashioned.

Like David, when you represent (even imperfectly) the heart, character, and priorities of Jesus, your Savior can make up for all your inadequacies as a leader. Do not let your imperfections as a Christian disqualify you as his representative. The imperfect King David pointed forward to the perfect Christ. Likewise, you, as an imperfect leader, can point backward to the perfect Master.

God needs you to bring his kingdom to bear in your sphere of influence. This is his call on Master Leaders. It is an obligation. It is a responsibility for all who call Jesus Master and who have been appointed as his shepherds.

Chapter Summary

To accomplish more, we need to do less. This is easier said than done, particularly for leaders of faith. Not only do we want to accomplish our own goals locally, we also want to honor God by building his kingdom globally. That is as challenging for the pastor of a local church as it is for the Christian leader in the marketplace. Master Leaders prioritize first what Jesus did. The challenge is to give his priorities pride of place in our own endeavors so that when we stand before him, we can honestly say to God, "Your majesty, my life's work was to build your kingdom, not my own." This requires taking action, which we will address in the next chapter.

TAKE ACTION ON FOCUSING PRIORITIES

Every effective leader knows this principle: do less to accomplish more. For the Christian leader, the stakes are much higher. We are not merely committed to the highest priorities of our own industry—whether a church, business, or nonprofit; we are also committed to God's priorities driving ours. The principles and teachings of Jesus provide a profound blueprint for leadership that transcends mere organizational success, aiming instead for a profound impact on the world around us. The two action steps below are designed not just to challenge you but also to change you. Engaging with these exercises is the first step toward embodying the kind of leader that can do less yet accomplish more by focusing on what truly matters.

Delegation Guide

Develop a Strategic Process for Delegation

Step #1: Identify tasks to be delegated. If you're going to delegate, you must eliminate. That's why your "Don't-Do" list may be more important than your "To-Do" list. These are items you're currently doing that you need to delegate to others so that you are only doing what only *you* can do. Begin by making a list of all your primary weekly tasks, no matter how small. Next, divide your list into four categories:

1) Tasks only you can do
2) Tasks others can do
3) Tasks that can be automated
4) Tasks that can be eliminated

Tasks that only you can do should be *very* few and should only revolve around vision and accountability to authority. None of these tasks should revolve around your ability. You may not be able to delegate certain levels of authority, but you *can* delegate any ability-based task. If you can't, then you have failed as a leader to adequately train your staff or to pass on strategic elements to those you lead.

Any task that *can* be automated *should* be automated immediately. With the rise of AI, we would be foolish not to investigate the burgeoning tools available for automation. Any task that is obsolete or ineffective should be eliminated as soon as you can communicate to the people who will be affected by this gap. Early in your career, you have to say yes to a lot of things to build your skills, reputation, and experience. But the further you advance, the more your success will be defined by your no rather than your yes.

Step #2: Identify the delegates. Start by creating Key Performance Indicators (KPIs). For each task, define measurable KPIs that will indicate the task's successful completion. Then, write the names of people you believe could accomplish each task at least 80 percent as well as you could. There will be a learning curve where you lose acceptable performance to achieve increased quality. Often, others can eventually outperform you. By empowering them for success, you draw the best out of them.

Step #3: Communicate specifically. Ensure you share with delegates these specific areas: a) the "why" of the task, b) expected outcomes with specific KPIs, c) deadlines broken down for each step of the task, d) available resources, including appropriate ways to ask for help or clarifying questions, and e) possible challenges and their solutions.

Step #4: Create automated training. There may be some items you cannot delegate right now because you have not yet trained anyone to accomplish them. Assign those items a thirty-, sixty-, and ninety-day window in which you (or someone on your team) will create an online, step-by-step training. Prioritize these training mechanisms to create more time for your future self to do what only you can do.

Step #5: Feedback loop. Establish a mechanism your delegate can use to update you on the progress of the task, using the KPIs as a guide. This will generally involve brief one-on-one check-ins (daily, weekly, or monthly, depending on the task) to discuss progress and challenges and to provide guidance. After completing each task, do a brief after-action report to identify what went well, where they could improve, and helpful alterations of the KPIs going forward. This may reveal gaps in the skills or knowledge of your delegate that you can augment to improve performance with training or resources (or both). Continue the follow-up meetings until the delegate reaches 95 percent proficiency.

Step #6: Affirmation and empowerment. Design systems of public recognition and affirmation. This doesn't necessarily mean financial reward. People are more motivated by verbal recognition and increased freedom and responsibility in the organization. Effective delegation is not primarily about offloading tasks but about empowering team members, fostering growth, and optimizing productivity. Your goal is not to make yourself more effective but to make your team more effective.

Priority Alignment

Integrate Your Daily Actions with God's Eternal Purpose

Start a note on your phone entitled "Tasks and Priorities." List all the tasks you accomplish in your leadership role. It may take a week or more to complete the list as things come across your inbox and calendar. Once you have a fairly comprehensive list, prioritize it as to what is most important to your church or organization.

Sit down and compare your list to the list of Jesus' priorities. Three times Jesus said, "I have come to . . . ." These are his life-purpose statements. One is in John, one is in Luke, and one is shared by Matthew and Mark:

- John 10:10, "I came that they may have life and have it abundantly."
- Luke 19:10, "For the Son of Man came to seek and to save the lost."
- Mark 10:45, "For even the Son of Man came not to be served but to serve, and to give his life as a ransom for many."

Though these three purpose statements of Jesus have obvious overlap, they certainly include Jesus' concern for our physical and social health, our mental and emotional health, and our spiritual health. As our Shepherd, he made our holistic well-being his priority:

1. Physical and social: loving the poor and disenfranchised (John 10:10; also Matt. 23:23; 25:35–40).
2. Mental and emotional: seeking and saving the lost—inclusion for outsiders (Luke 19:10).
3. Spiritual: laying down his life as a ransom and asking us to do the same as Master Leaders (Matt. 20:28; Mark 10:45).

How many of your priorities do or could align with Jesus' top three priorities for building the kingdom? Try to identify ways in which your organizational priorities could include one of these three aspects of building the kingdom of God. Draw a line between your list of priorities and Jesus' priorities. Then brainstorm specific actions you could take that would integrate Jesus' priorities into those of your organization.

11

TAKE ACTION

The year 1995 was a magical moment for sports—not because of the popularity of rugby in South Africa (which was huge), but because of its impact on human rights. It's a crazy story. New Zealand was a powerhouse in the sport and the clear favorite for the World Cup. South Africa, the host country, found themselves in the finals, which set the nation buzzing. The newly elected president of South Africa showed up wearing the #6 jersey of team flanker Francois Pienaar. Normally, there would have been nothing striking about that, except that Nelson Mandela, recently released from twenty-seven years in prison, was Black. Rugby was notably a white man's sport. For some, it was even a symbol of apartheid, of which Mandela was a fierce opponent. As a result, many of Mandela's supporters took offense to his public show of support for a sport that, for them, symbolized oppression.

But Mandela knew there was something bigger at play than rugby. He understood that unity required acceptance and understanding that went both ways. Mandela's mission to unify the country drove his actions. This singular event at the finals had such unprecedented power for racial reconciliation that actor/director Clint Eastwood shared the story in 2009 through the box-office sensation *Invictus.* Mandela's mission was merely wishful thinking until he put feet to his faith. That's the point. Mission matters, but only after it grows legs. Mandela had to *do* the right thing, not just *say* the right thing.

That's why Master Leaders have a strong bias for action. Before we look at Jesus' final call to action, Jeff will help us think through our own leadership bias to be doers rather than just thinkers.

What Do We Do?

At the end of the day, leaders know how to get stuff done. Not just *any* stuff, but the *right* stuff. To make this happen, leaders must master the value of action, because action drives results, and results make impact. If we have created a compelling vision, constructed an effective strategy, and narrowed our focus but never pulled the trigger on action, we will fail to accomplish the mission. We are simply daydreaming! Master Leaders know how to mobilize others to take action that yields fruit.

Successful leaders tend to have a strong bias for action, which simply means they're eager to act swiftly and with conviction. Warning: the key to this principle is that you are taking the *appropriate* action, not just any action. Many times, we as leaders fall into the trap of telling ourselves, "Don't just stand there; do something!" This causes us to take actions we may not have fully thought through or that we may even regret later. As leadership experts sometimes say, flipping this saying, "Don't just do something; stand there!" In this reversal of thought, we are reminded that sometimes our job as leaders is to pause before we act. We need to take the time to really think about it before we take random actions; we need to make sure it is the *right* action. For many of us, this one is tough, particularly if we are Type A leaders.

We've all seen (and probably worked with) leaders who love to act and act quickly. They're guilty of "fire, ready, aim." They can't stand to pause and seek wise counsel before taking the next step. They just don't have the patience to wait. Conversely, Master Leaders know the difference between *movement* and *motion*. Motion is any activity that makes things happen. It can move us in any direction. Movement, however, takes us in the direction of the destination.

Think about a football running back who takes the ball from the quarterback, and instead of running north or south, he runs all around the backfield, eluding the defense by running east and west, exhausting a ton of energy and not moving the ball down the field. This may create temporary excitement for the fans, but in the end, the play is not considered a success.

One simple hack to help avoid falling into this trap of "fire, ready, aim" is to ask our peers or team members a simple question: "Hey, can you check my thinking on this?" The term "check my thinking" is a great way to create a simple pause. This pause doesn't mean we're unsure about what step to take next or that we don't have confidence in our decision. It is a simple and easy, yet humble, way to ask those around us if they think our train of thought makes sense. It brings others into the process before we take an action we might later regret. I have found this to be a very helpful way to seek input while avoiding analysis paralysis or bringing too many people into a process that needs to happen with speed and pace.

Many of us have been guilty of juking around in the backfield, feeling good that we are moving, making decisions, and getting things done. Yet in the end, we burned a lot of time and resources, potentially exhausting our team without making forward progress. To be a leader of action, we first must be sure that we're clear on our destination (our vision), that we have chosen the correct strategies, that we have focused on the vital few objectives that will make the greatest impact, and that we are able to prioritize and make decisions that lead to fruitful action.

Jeff's advice above is spot on. Having a strong bias for action is a great practice for a Master Leader, but ensuring that action will create movement and not just motion is what really matters. To that end, let's look at Jesus' call to action in what church leaders call the "Great Commission." This was Jesus' final command before leaving earth.

The Great Commission

As we've already established, Jesus' vision was the kingdom of God. His mission was the global expansion of his followers. Both are captured in Christ's final command to his disciples, called the Great Commission: "All authority in heaven and on earth has been given to me. Go therefore and make disciples of all nations, baptizing them in the name of the Father and of the Son and of the Holy Spirit, teaching them to observe all that I have commanded you" (Matt. 28:18–20).

This last command—a call to action—must be our first priority. This single sentence contains nuclear power. It is a small package with global potential. In English, there are four action verbs in the sentence: 1) go, 2) make disciples, 3) baptize, and 4) teach. In the original Greek, however, there is only one verb. The other three are participles that support the one verb. That one verb, our singular priority, is to "make disciples."

Jesus's last command—a call to action—must be our first priority.

The three participles are the means of accomplishing the singular priority. *Going* into all the world (or literally to every ethnic group) is a precursor to making disciples. *Baptizing* is the initiation of the disciples—a ceremonial death and rebirth symbolizing a pledge of loyalty to the king. *Teaching* is the means of training disciples. Together, these three actions make disciples. They are *how* we accomplish our mission. For a Christian, making disciples *is* our mission.

Let me be clear here. Making disciples is the mission of every church and every Christian. However, not every church (or every Christian) has the same strategic actions for accomplishing the mission. Each local church and each individual Christian have unique opportunities, resources, needs, and advocates. Christian leaders must discover and lead toward a focused endemic mission through the local church. Though the Great Commission is global, the local church mission is local and idiosyncratic. It should align with who we are, where we are, and how God wired us. That means we need to ask, "Why did God give us these resources in this place at this time?" What can you *do* that is unique to your organization that would supplement and support the overall work of God in your world? In other words, how can you put feet to your faith to make disciples?

How Do I Make Disciples?

There are shelves of books on discipleship theory. All kinds of authors advocate and argue for various approaches. Most, however, lean into ideas to be taught more than actions to implement. I believe that most of these ideas can be helpful. Many of these books are insightful. Nonetheless, right here, right now, let's not overcomplicate the issue. Bottom line: a disciple is a "learner"—a student, so to speak. However, the particular type of learning the Jewish culture had in mind had less to do with information and was much more about transformation. It was about behavior, not books—action over ideation. It's what we would call apprenticeship or mentoring. The disciple would follow, imitate, and replicate the actions a mentor would model.

Move from Hearing to Doing, from Coming to Going

If you catalog all the uses of "disciple" throughout Jesus' ministry, you'll discover precisely how one followed Jesus in practice. It required using five different body parts: ears, eyes, mouth, hands, and feet. Typically, they came in pairs.

Stage 1 Discipleship: Eyes and Feet. Jesus called his disciples to "come and see." He asked them to move from where they were to where he was and observe his actions. This is not so different from what parents, coaches, and managers ask of their apprentices—come and see. Rather than going to a coffee shop to have a Bible study with disciples, we invite them to tag along on ministry ventures. Again, whether you're a vocational church leader or not, bring an apprentice to visit the sick, serve the homeless, or go on a mission trip. Ask them to observe an evangelistic encounter, a counseling appointment, or a strategic planning session. It's not what we *say* that makes the most profound impact. It's what we *do* to execute the mission. That's what our disciples see—our actions! What you have been doing naturally, almost reflexively, for decades is still a mystery for newcomers. Show them how to do the things you can do without blinking or thinking.

Stage 2 Discipleship: Ears and Mouth. These came into play when Jesus' disciples listened to him preach. They were not merely absorbing style or even content. They were integrating his priorities, learning what was important to Jesus. Then Jesus asked them to go out and preach the message of the kingdom of God. He asked them to use their personalities, gifts, and experiences to act on his behalf, representing his priorities to those far from God. That's discipleship in a nutshell.

Teaching theological truths has value, of course. But very few people, statistically, will ever be called to execute the spiritual gift of teaching biblical content. Yet every Christ-follower is expected to share their story of the transformational impact Jesus has made in their lives. In short, everyone who has heard about Jesus should be talking about Jesus to those who don't know Jesus.

Stage 3 Discipleship: Hands and Feet. At this stage, we go and do. Jesus sent out his disciples to accomplish the same healing ministry and social construction he modeled. Jesus said it himself: "Truly, truly, I say to you, whoever believes in me will also do the works that I do; and greater works than these will he do, because I am going to the Father" (John 14:12).

Wait, did Jesus say that we would do *more* than *he* did? He did! And we are, in fact, doing more today than Jesus did when he was on earth. This, of course, doesn't mean we're dying for people's sins. That is the exclusive role of our Savior. Nor does it mean that we will miraculously raise the dead or cleanse lepers. We are, however, healing more people than he ever did using medicine, clinics, and mission trips. We are rescuing more children through after-school programs, foster care initiatives, human trafficking disruption, and orphanages. We are liberating more women through literacy training, marriage retreats, compassionate support of widows, and job training.

Pastoring a church is a narrow band of what disciples are called to do. That's why pastors must lead and not merely teach. Perhaps the single most important role of a pastor is to apprentice non-pastoral professionals to use their vocation as a ministry and to turn their home into a church. Pastors must mentor community leaders to make Jesus' kingdom the preoccupation of their occupations. When the entire body makes Jesus famous where they live, work, and play, we will be on track to complete the Great Commission.

Discipleship, like leadership, must prefer action over thinking. That means we're not just *talking* about implementing God's kingdom. We're not just *praying* that God's will be done on earth as it is in heaven. We are doing something to bring God's kingdom from heaven to earth by strategically implementing a distinctive mission to respond to the gifts, calling, experiences, and resources that God has put at our disposal. Give priority to action over ideation, doing over talking.

In short, we must move discipleship from *hearing* to *doing* and from *coming* to *going*. Like a business meeting, a Bible study must become a mechanism for action. It is the huddle, not the play. Everyone who comes to learn must be coached to go and perform. If not, study alone will likely create more arrogance than competence in disciples. If we measure our spiritual success by what we know rather than by what we do, we are in danger of what the apostle Paul warned: "'Knowledge puffs up, but love builds up" (1 Cor. 8:1).

Chapter Summary

The Great Commission is Jesus' final command. For the Master Leader, it must become our first priority. Though the commission includes going, baptizing, and teaching, the core is making disciples. For far too long, Christian leaders have focused on the teaching side. But making a disciple is more about apprenticing a follower of Jesus than developing a budding theologian. As leaders, we have a bias for action. We have to. So let's act by raising up doers for the kingdom more than philosophers or theologians. We must move those we coach from watching and thinking to going and doing. This will require the Master Leader to do more than talk. We must mentor other young leaders to lead like the Master. How does one go about that? Well, that is the subject of the next and final chapter: mentoring.

TAKE ACTION ON TAKING ACTION

Master Leaders have a bias for action over talking, but often that is hampered by meetings with people who want to prolong valued time with their leader (whether personal or corporate). They love ideation with the leader because it feels like affirmation (to both of you, frankly). So how do we focus on action in an environment where conversation, hesitation, and procrastination can lead to stagnation? Adopting a proactive stance is crucial for any leader aspiring to make a significant impact. Here are some concrete suggestions for creating a bias for action within the organization.

Action Orientation

Foster a Culture with a Bias for Action

Not all of these suggestions will be top priority for you. Select two to implement this week and two more to implement in the next quarter.

- *Identify the purpose of each meeting.* In an email prior to the meeting, identify whether it is a meeting for delivering information, making a decision, creating a product, or establishing a plan of action. Each of these kinds of meetings requires different inputs. We get bogged down when an information meeting turns into a creation meeting and the product gets redesigned.
- *Only invite contributors to meetings.* If a person is not needed for the meeting, they can merely be informed about the purpose and decisions of the meeting through an email.
- *Reduce the length of the meeting.* More often than not, meetings will fill the allotted scheduled time. So give them less space. One idea is to have meetings of random length, such as seventeen or twenty-three minutes. This sends a subtle message that we will stick to the deliberate time.
- *Implement the "parking lot."* Any item that's not part of the agenda or cannot be clearly addressed should be pushed to the "parking lot" for later follow-up.
- *Follow up each meeting with clear tasks.* After each meeting, send an email that reiterates who's responsible for each action item coming out of the meeting, the due date for each action item, and who will follow up with the responsible person and through what mechanism (email, one-on-one, phone call, etcetera). There are now AI apps you can use, even on a smartphone, to record the meeting and automate all the necessary follow-up.
- *Empower decision-making at lower levels of the organization.* The further you push down a yes, the more agile your organization will become.
- *Experiment with a project management strategy.* There are some agile tactical strategies such as Scrum or Kanban that enhance flexibility and responsiveness. (Both are worth looking up if they are unfamiliar to you.)

- *Foster a "fail fast" mindset.* Create an environment where failure is seen as a learning opportunity. Work hard to reduce the fear of taking action and encourage more risk-taking.
- *Set an unrealistic deadline for a project.* Push the team to sprint for a short season. They can go further faster than they imagine. Celebrate the achievement even if the target is not hit.
- *Seek broad input for a perplexing problem.* Collect the craziest, most innovative, and sometimes impossible solutions from every level of the organization regardless of roles or job descriptions. See what sticks.
- *Don't entertain problems that don't come with a solution.* Refusing to hear about a problem without an accompanying proposed solution helps set a culture of action over reflection.

Ownership Orientation

Foster a Mindset of Personal Responsibility

Work *on* the organization you lead—not *for* the organization. How? Take a walking tour of your organization, clipboard in hand. Make a note of every change you would make if you owned the organization. You might even invite a secret shopper to do this for you (see the Secret Shopper exercise from chapter 6). Prioritize your list into items that fall within your sphere of influence. Set out to find solutions to problems that would make life easier for your direct report(s). To use Clay Scroggins's term from his book *How to Lead When You're Not In Charge,* create an "oasis of excellence" in your own area of influence.[18] Make your space a model of innovation following in the direction of the organization's missional priorities.

When you act like an owner rather than a manager, several things happen almost immediately. First, you invest resources rather than spend them. It's easier for employees than employers to waste resources, just as it's easier for children to waste their parents' money. Second, you focus on the organization rather than on any individual. You don't do what is best for you but for the company. You don't do what's best for a friend but for the organization. You don't consider the pain of a person first but the pain of the team. This doesn't mean you lack compassion. Far from it. Your compassion is for many, not just one, and you won't put up with anything or anyone damaging the health of the team that accomplishes the mission. Third, you focus on the future, not just the present. Rather than working to help programs and people survive, you are willing to change both people and programs to help the community thrive. After all, you have a vision of a preferred future.

12

MENTOR LEADERS

Bill Walsh may be the most effective football coach in history. He transformed the San Francisco 49ers into the most dominant team in the 1980s (winning three Super Bowls). But that is only part of his contribution. He also invested in the next generation of winning coaches. Mike Holmgren, one of Walsh's assistants, became the head coach of the Green Bay Packers, winning Super Bowl XXXI with the Packers and later leading the Seattle Seahawks to their first Super Bowl appearance in franchise history. Holmgren mentored Andy Reid, who became the head coach of the Philadelphia Eagles from 1999 to 2012 and had one Super Bowl appearance with the team. After becoming the head coach of the Kansas City Chiefs, however, Reid took home the title three times. Reid mentored Doug Pederson, who took the Philadelphia Eagles to their first Super Bowl victory in 2017.

Walsh's legacy illustrates a powerful principle in leadership: great leaders seldom rise in a vacuum. Consider the greatest philosophers in history: Socrates mentored Plato, who mentored Aristotle, who mentored Alexander the Great. What a legacy of influence. Likewise, during the American Revolution, you had a conglomerate of politicians of renown: George Washington, Thomas Jefferson, Alexander Hamilton, and Benjamin Franklin. All were contemporaries learning from one another and making an exponential impact due to their interaction. It is true in every arena: Master Leaders mentor great leaders. If you want recognition, win. If you want to be remembered, raise up winners. Before we examine the biblical model of mentors, I've asked Jeff to offer his own reflections as a C-level leader about raising up the next generation of leaders.

Master Leaders mentor great leaders. To be remembered, raise up winners.

Who Do We Raise Up?

Simply put, there is no success without a successor. This is a timeless principle of leadership. We are the result of many other leaders who have gone before us and have chosen to make the investment in us to help us get to where we are today. The phrase "I am a self-made person" is nearly always a gross exaggeration of the truth. The fact is, none of us got here without others taking the time to invest in us. We are the product of many other people. So let's look at legacy—what we leave for those who follow us.

When we hear the term "legacy," we often think of money and assets. This is, of course, one dimension of leaving a legacy. But Master Leaders have the opportunity to leave a legacy of leadership, to invest in those who follow in our leadership footprints. We set the stage for those we've had the privilege to lead to be even better leaders than we were. Some might say, "I am too busy to invest in future leaders." But when we are too busy focusing on our own success, we forfeit our future significance.

I was a college track athlete, and my very favorite race was the 400-meter relay. It wasn't just about having the four fastest runners on the track. In fact, in most cases the race was won or lost in the handoff. I think this principle is the same with our ministries, nonprofits, and businesses. The big picture is all about the handoff. Who comes after us? Who will ensure the vision continues to be pursued? Who will be able to learn from the scar tissue we have experienced over the last several decades so they don't have to relearn some of those painful lessons?

Investing and mentoring the next generation of leaders is not optional for Master Leaders. It is an obligation. We must share with others what we learned, how we solved difficult challenges, and how we were able to stay faithful to the assignment God gave us without giving in or giving up. Even the great apostles needed mentors. Barnabas poured into Paul, who, having seen the importance of mentoring firsthand, made it a point to pour into Timothy. God did not create us to do this life alone; we need each other, and we need community. I have had mentors over the years who have invested their time and talents to allow me the opportunity to be ready to raise my leadership game when the coach told me it was time to step up and lead.

When I left a successful career at a multibillion-dollar global technology company to pursue my first CEO role at a private equity start-up company, to say I was intimidated and anxious about the weight of the role would have been a significant understatement. Shortly after taking on this new role, I received a phone call from the CEO of my prior company asking if I was interested in coming back; when I explained to him that the new job was harder than expected but also more rewarding than I could have imagined, he then quickly changed the direction of the conversation and said, "Well, if you aren't coming back, I guess I will come with you." This uber-successful Fortune 200 CEO was gracious enough to join my company's board of directors after he retired for the sole purpose of mentoring me as a first-time CEO. After nearly five years of lessons, mistakes, and insights, we successfully sold the company to another investor group. Without his mentorship and selfless investment in me, this journey would never have been possible.

To be invested in by a leader who has gone before you is an amazing gift. Being the one to mentor and pour into those who come after you is, in my opinion, an even greater gift. Recently, we said goodbye to an employee named Ray who had been with our church for seven years. For the last three of those years, I had taken on the role of mentoring him by meeting with him monthly, not to talk about work projects or performance feedback, but to talk specifically about how to develop him as a leader, communicator, and—eventually—a father. During his last week, we had Ray's farewell lunch and showered him with verbal gifts of affirmation, memories, and encouragement. Ray left me a letter in an envelope that I read after he departed. I'll share the first part of that letter: "Words can't express how thankful I am for you, nor could they do justice articulating the impact you've had on my life over the past three years—truly immeasurable."

I don't share that to brag about the letter or even hint that I am a model leader. I simply share it with you to say that I have had many successes in my business career and have made investors tens of millions of dollars, but those achievements don't hold a candle to the words he wrote to me in that letter. Being able to mentor others and have an impact in their life is our legacy. We owe it to our Lord and those who come after us to give back generously what has been given to us. My life verse is Luke 12:48: "Everyone to whom much was given, of him much will be required."

Mentoring: Move from Teaching to Coaching

Like Jeff's story illustrates, Master Leaders give generously of their time, talent, and treasures to ensure their legacy continues long after their assignment is complete. Our best chance to mentor well is to follow the leadership example of the heroes of the faith. In the Bible, we find multiple mentor-mentee relationships. Jethro mentored his son-in-law Moses. Even though Moses was the adopted son of Pharaoh and the leader of the nation, Jethro took him aside to counsel him about his lack of delegation in leadership—a great gift, not just to Moses but to the nation. Moses then mentored Joshua. This young man of faith had all the right stuff but lacked courage. Moses infused him with confidence to lead twelve turbulent tribes to take the territory that God had promised them. Jethro shows us that you don't need formal titles or power to impact the leadership of the next generation. Furthermore, your impact is not just in those you mentor, but in those that they, in turn, raise up as leaders.

Eli, though a failure as a father and a priest, offered invaluable experience and wisdom to young Samuel, who went on to become the kingmaker of Israel. Samuel anointed both Saul and David. Likewise, Naomi, a refugee widow, mentored Ruth, her daughter-in-law. Because of their loving relationship and Naomi's life-coaching, Ruth was adopted into Judaism and is one of the four women highlighted in the genealogy of Jesus. These examples show us that our own failure or personal deficit does not prohibit us from making major contributions to others' leadership through mentoring.

Mordecai mentored his young cousin, Esther, the winner of a national beauty pageant. It wasn't a frivolous beauty contest; there was survival from a genocide at stake. She became a savior of her nation and is still celebrated today by Jews worldwide in the festival of Purim each spring. We can have world-changing influence in the shadows when we put others center stage.

Elijah mentored Elisha. This young prophet had the audacity to pray to God for a double portion of Elijah's power. God gave it to him. You can count the miracles yourself; they are double those of Elijah. The two prophets are commonly confused or combined, demonstrating how your mentoring actually extends and expands your own leadership legacy. Though Elisha did more miracles, Elijah is far more renowned in Jewish literature and lore. That matters to us as Master Leaders because it proves that investing in others actually does come back to roost in your own nest. Or to quote the common promise of Scripture, if you humble yourself, God will exalt you (Prov. 29:23; Matt. 23:12; Luke 14:11; 18:14; James 4:10; 1 Pet. 5:5–6).

Jesus, of course, modeled mentoring with the Twelve, even prioritizing three leaders among the group: Peter, James, and John. Peter and John went on to write a good bit of the New Testament. Peter's disciple Mark was responsible for what many assume is the first Gospel written. John, of course, added the final Gospel bearing his name as well as the last book of the Bible, Revelation. The lesson here is clear: what you pour into others, they will magnify.

The most famous mentoring relationship in the Bible is between Paul and Timothy. Yet we would be remiss not to mention that Jesus also mentored Paul for three years in Arabia (Gal. 1:17–18). There is a legacy of leadership here. Moreover, while we have several books written to Timothy and Titus (Paul's mentees), we also have two substantial documents from Luke, another of Paul's disciples, who wound up writing more words of the New Testament than his mentor. When we delve into their biographies, there are four mentoring axioms to be learned.

Axiom #1: Leadership begins with submission. Timothy's journey with Paul started by submitting to outpatient surgery (Acts 16:3). We are most struck by the physical pain of a twentysomething going through circumcision. However, for Timothy, the deeper issue, by far, was marking his body, in Greek culture, in such a way that would permanently bring him scorn. He submitted to this, however, because he respected Paul's leadership. After that, Timothy was an errand boy. He delivered letters to the churches Paul planted and then returned with a report and a collection he had received from the church. Though Timothy must have heard Paul teach a lot, he also spent much time away from his mentor, carrying out menial tasks to build Paul's network and effectiveness. *Lesson:* raise up leaders who demonstrate humility before ability. Going back to our very first leadership lesson, integrity of character is the foundation of trust.

Axiom #2: You cannot train a disciple to listen if they don't know the language. Implementing our spiritual gifts effectively requires an apprenticeship. The first thing we must learn is how to hear the voice of God (Acts 16:6–10). In non-church vocations, that is equivalent to reading the signs of the times—business and cultural trends—which also stems from acute listening to the Spirit of God. Paul will later exhort Timothy to continue to pray for that same foundational skill of hearing the Spirit and following God's will (1 Tim. 2:1–2, 8). Only after learning to hear God can we learn to speak for him (2 Tim. 1:13–14; 2:2; 4:2). Training disciples to hear God's voice may be the most important lesson a Master Leader can coach. And, as I've learned in my decades of pastoral experience, the voice of God most often is the clearest through a mentor's voice.

Training disciples to hear God is a vital lesson Master Leaders teach.

Axiom #3: Personal progress is tied to loyalty to leaders. Timothy spent a lot of time away from Paul running errands. This must have been a frustrating season where he felt like he needed to be learning or reaching his potential. Others were given the limelight. Nonetheless, in this season of Timothy's life, he adopted Paul's priorities. Even at the end of Paul's life, when all others had abandoned him, Timothy's loyalties to Paul made him the primary choice for the great apostle to ask to carry out his errands, even the most seemingly tedious ones (see 2 Tim. 4:13). *Lesson:* don't look for talent above loyalty. Mentor those who are loyal to the organization, or in the case of a Master Leader, the kingdom of God. Talent can be trained far easier than character. This leads to the final axiom.

Axiom #4: Trust is built more by long loyalty than raw talent. Though Timothy is notably silent (or absent) in Philippi, Thessalonica, and Berea, he finally got the opportunity to join Paul's teaching team for the first time in Corinth (2 Cor. 1:19). This would become the launching pad for his primary assignment in Ephesus (1 Tim. 4:11–13). He was, however, more than a teacher. He modeled the Christian life he taught about (1 Tim. 4:14–16; cf. 5:1–16; 2 Tim. 4:5) just as Paul had (Acts 20:32–35). While not all of us will teach with words, we will teach with our lives. What are people learning from how you live? Paul had a string of mentees in addition to Timothy. Silas, Luke, Priscilla, Aquila, and Crispus are some of the more notable names. Timothy was charged to do the same thing (1 Tim. 3:1–12). Leaders tend to offer opportunities for loyalty more than ability. *Lesson:* you are not merely mentoring a future leader; you are mentoring a future mentor. Paul summarized it well in the last letter he ever wrote: "What you have heard from me in the presence of many witnesses entrust to faithful men, who will be able to teach others also" (2 Tim. 2:2).

Chapter Summary

If leadership is influence, then a Master Leader is more interested in building a legacy than a brand. When all is said and done, your leadership will not be counted by the number of digits in your trust but the number of disciples you entrusted. Jesus is, without a close second, the most influential leader of human history. When the Master gets hold of you, you become a Master Leader who mentors Master Leaders, leaving an eternal legacy.

TAKE ACTION ON MENTORING LEADERS

Making disciples is the core of our commission. Without it, there is a potentially short shelf life of your legacy. The following exercises will help you identify how to pour into others who will build beyond you. Mentoring has the double benefit of protecting the future of the organization as well as shaping today your primary mission. For those who are nervous about mentoring, or perhaps are inexperienced, these exercises may seem daunting—or worse, an overwhelming imposition of time. However, if you have led well at any level, you realize your greatest achievement is not in your accomplishments but in your investments. It is through the deliberate act of mentoring that we perpetuate our values and enlarge the parameters of our vision. More than that, mentoring is the mechanism by which we refine our own character and leadership capacities.

Mentor Assessment

Analyze What It Takes for You to Invest in Others

For many, mentoring seems like a daunting task. We don't feel qualified to make our life a model for others. But if you think about those who made the greatest impact in your life, it was their simple presence, not their impressive performance, that mattered most. You can do that!

The Mentor Assessment invites you to reflect on the individuals who have significantly impacted your life across various stages. By identifying the qualities and actions that made these mentors influential, you gain insights into the mentoring style that resonates with you and those you lead. By recognizing the simplicity of impactful mentoring—often marked by presence rather than performance—you will be inspired to up your own mentoring game and make a more meaningful impact in the lives of others with actions you can choose right now. Remember, mentoring is the pinnacle of becoming a Master Leader. Take your mentoring journey to the next level by downloading this exercise at TheMasterLeader.com/tools.

Mentor Group

Cultivate a Circle of Future Master Leaders

Though there is no single right way to mentor future leaders, it starts with selection. If you are doing professional mentoring for a potential replacement or private mentoring through a crisis, one-on-one mentoring is preferable. Virtually all other mentoring, in my experience, is better done in a group. Group mentoring will not only multiply your investment of time but also will allow each member to feed off the others beyond what you could do alone. Groups between four and six are small enough to be intimate and transparent but not so small that one missing member creates an awkward meeting.

Choosing the right people for the group is mission critical. My litmus test is threefold: 1) These individuals must have high capacity and high emotional intelligence. 2) They must entertain me. Yes, I said it out loud. If they are not life-giving to me, I'm not giving my life to them. That's not selfish; it's self-aware. I know my limits. 3) They must blend well with each other. The synergy of the group is paramount to the success of the group feeding each other. Finding the right combination of people may take six to nine months. It's worth waiting for.

Once you have your group, what do you do? Nothing. Well, almost nothing. One of my hard-and-fast rules is that I am not responsible for the group. They are to bring me their questions, challenges, and growth plans. If they don't own it, it will not stick. We meet weekly or monthly, depending on the group. We pray together every time we meet, and we talk through their plans, challenges, and dreams. Once or twice during the year, we play, eat, and work together. These alternate environments reveal different strengths and weaknesses of the mentees. In every environment, we have deliberately significant conversations. Those conversations lead to the magic—when you discover where they need to grow and then challenge them with actual growth tasks, as Paul did with Timothy. *The talk time must lead to assignments* that will push their limits and put into action the talents lying latent within them.

Oh, and there is one last thing. You speak life into them. You tell them what you see in them. Often, young men and women hear the voice of God through the words of Master Leaders. The most powerful thing you have to offer them is a view of their life through the windshield rather than the rearview mirror. This is of inestimable value.

THE CHALLENGE OF A MASTER LEADER

It is an unassailable historical fact that no human being has made more of an impact on humanity than Jesus of Nazareth. Moreover, his impact has been disproportionately large in areas that affect human flourishing: education, ethics, science, medicine, literature, music, architecture, liberation from slavery, alleviation of poverty, and protection of women, children, refugees, and the oppressed. As worshipers of Jesus Christ, we look to him as Savior. That is eternally true. But even now, and even in a secular society, Jesus' words of wisdom and integrity of character loom large. He is an example worth following for the advancement of the human species. This is fairly common ground, regardless of one's religious, political, or cultural position. Yet for Christians, he is more. He is more than a Savior; he is our Lord.

That means his leadership example is not merely a suggestion. It is a mandate for modeling. The way Jesus led, which led to the greatest global impact, is a template for us to build our own leadership superstructure upon.

While the world can talk about "integrity" as ethical consistency, we know it comes from an identity derived from the Father's approval. Worldly leaders (and Christian leaders who follow worldly models) have failed colossally in integrity. That's because they don't have the internal resources that Jesus gave us to live in and through the approval of our heavenly Father.

Although secular leadership literature lauds servant leadership, it doesn't have the foundation to uphold it. Servant leadership originated with Jesus. It is a conviction of faith that if we humble ourselves God will exalt us. When you take God out of the equation, the infrastructure of servant leadership disintegrates, leaving you with platitudes rather than action plans.

It is the model of Jesus that builds integrity and servanthood—the foundation of stewardship. It is precisely our embodied theology of God's ownership of everything that gives us the tools to steward God's gifts, whether people, time, talent, or resources. Master Leaders have a whole different mindset because of Jesus' counterintuitive model.

This is clearly seen in the consistency we build through prayer and Sabbath. These practices are outwardly focused on God. The secular equivalent is meditation and relaxation, which are inwardly focused. Meditation features emptying your mind, and relaxation focuses on getting away. In contrast, prayer is about filling your mind with God's thoughts, and Sabbath is about connecting with God and others. Is it any wonder, then, that Master Leaders are able to live more consistently and lead more relentlessly?

These are the tools that empower Master Leaders to care with the same selfless sacrifice of Jesus. It is not the sympathy of wearing a ribbon for a cause or subscribing to cancel culture. It is taking up a cross and laying down our lives for those who may not deserve it but most need it. This is the path to significance. In a paradoxical study at the University of Chicago, they found that, though pastors are among the lowest paid occupations for the hours they put in and the education they attained, they yet rank among the happiest people on the planet.[19]

Jesus' model of love also makes us the nimblest leaders. After all, we are not fixated on our own needs and desires but on caring for the sheep that God has put in our care. We are far more motivated to move, to be alert, and to alter course when we are shepherding the flock of God for his glory rather than our own comfort, recognition, or reward.

These core characteristics of Jesus, when they grow in us, are the fertile soul fit for creating culture in the organizations we lead. The more we look like Jesus, the more others will want what we have. A model that mirrors Jesus (albeit imperfectly) is a compelling enticement to culture creation. Who doesn't want to live like that? Who doesn't want to love like that?

From such a Christlike culture rises a vision of a desirable future. Even in a secular organization, a Christocentric vision impels people to action. They may not have words for it or a theology under it, but bringing a bit of heaven to earth is an intoxicating enticement. We all have a God-shaped hole in our hearts. We were designed by our Creator to partner with him in making a beautiful world out of the earth he put under our feet.

Our strategy, like his, is to shepherd those he has entrusted us to lead. Like a shepherd, we lead, feed, heal, and protect. And when the flock is well-fed, resting beside quiet waters, the shepherd writes psalms to God because this sensation of significance is a more compelling reward by far than fame or fortune. We were made for this. *You* were made for this.

So it is time now, Master Leader, for you to focus in on your highest priorities, fulfilling your highest calling. It's time to mobilize the troops to take action. Whether you are a pastor or a marketplace leader, you are God's leader, caring for his flock. Our prayer is not merely that you would take them to a desired destination, bringing a bit of heaven to earth, but also that you would raise up leaders, perhaps using this very book, to extend your leadership to a generation yet to be born.

NOTES

1. John Maxwell, *Developing the Leaders Around You: How to Help Others Reach Their Full Potential* (Nashville, TN: Thomas Nelson, 1995), 6.

2. James Kouzes and Barry Posner, *The Leadership Challenge: How to Make Extraordinary Things Happen in Organizations*, 5th ed. (San Francisco: Jossey-Bass, 2012), 38.

3. In Bill George, Peter Sims, Andrew McLean, and Diana Mayer, "Discovering Your Authentic Leadership," in *HBR's 10 Must Reads on Leadership* (Boston: HBR, 2011), 168.

4. Chip Heath and Dan Heath, *The Power of Moments: Why Certain Experiences Have Extraordinary Impact* (New York: Simon & Schuster, 2017), 12–29. The authors observe that these moments can be far more powerful than much more extended investments if we are able to elevate the moment with true connection.

5. David Kinnaman and Aly Hawkins, *You Lost Me: Why Young Christians Are Leaving Church . . . and Rethinking Faith* (Grand Rapids, MI: Baker, 2011), 17.

6. Jim Loehr and Tony Schwartz, *The Power of Full Engagement: Managing Energy, Not Time, Is the Key to High Performance and Personal Renewal* (New York: Free Press, 2003), 14.

7. Loehr and Schwartz, *Power of Full Engagement*, 40. They go on to cite a word in Japanese, *karoshi*, that means "death from overwork," which is responsible for 10,000 deaths a year in Japan.

8. Henry Cloud, *Trust: Knowing When to Give It, When to Withhold It, How to Earn It, and How to Fix It When It Gets Broken* (Nashville, TN: Worthy, 2023), 41–120.

9. Craig Groeschel (@craiggroeschel), X (formerly known as Twitter), Jan 5, 2017, twitter.com/craiggroeschel/status/817155247290351618.

10. James Clear, *Atomic Habits: An Easy & Proven Way to Build Good Habits & Break Bad Ones* (New York: Avery, 2018), 24.

11. Clear, *Atomic Habits*, 186.

12. Chris Voss and Tahl Raz, *Never Split the Difference: Negotiating as If Your Life Depended on It* (New York: Harper Collins, 2016), 198.

13. Andy Stanley, *Deep and Wide: Creating Churches Unchurched People Love to Attend* (Grand Rapids, MI: Zondervan, 2016), 268.

14. Brad Lomenick, *The Catalyst Leader: 8 Essentials for Becoming a Change Maker* (Nashville, TN: Thomas Nelson, 2013), 43.

15. Patrick Lencioni, *The Advantage: Why Organizational Health Trumps Everything Else in Business* (San Francisco: Jossey Bass, 2012), 40–44.

16. Samuel Chand says, "You'll grow only to the threshold of your pain." See *Leadership Pain: The Classroom for Growth* (Nashville: Thomas Nelson, 2015), 15.

17. Stephen Covey, *The 7 Habits of Highly Effective People: Powerful Lessons in Personal Change* (New York: Simon & Schuster, 1989), 170.

18. Clay Scroggins, *How to Lead When You're Not in Charge* (Grand Rapids, MI: Zondervan, 2017), 34.

19. Chand, *Leadership Pain*, 51.

ABOUT THE AUTHORS

Mark E. Moore, PhD, has been a teaching pastor at Christ's Church of the Valley in Phoenix, Arizona, since 2012. Prior to that, he was a professor of New Testament at Ozark Christian College in Joplin, Missouri. He is noted for his passionate teaching and writing to make Jesus famous. Much of his material is available free online at markmoore.org. He and his bride live in Peoria, Arizona, and celebrate time with their two grown children, who serve in ministry, and their seven grandchildren.

With contributions by **Jeff Osborne**, who has served in the role of executive pastor at Christ's Church of the Valley since 2020. Prior to that, he was the CEO of Accumen, a private equity-backed national healthcare transformation company. He was also the chief performance officer at Accenture, a global consulting, technology, and outsourcing company. Jeff has held several other chief operating officer roles and a variety of other executive-level leadership roles over the past three decades. He and his wife of thirty years live in Peoria, Arizona, and have three adult children.